Letts

GCSE

VISUAL REVISION GUIDE

SUCCESS

BUSINESS STUDIES

Author

David Floyd

CONTENTS

OUR ECONOMY AND BUSINESS

INSIDE AND OUTSIDE THE BUSINESS

PEOPLE IN BUSINESS

FINANCE IN BUSINESS

MAKING THE PRODUCTS

SELLING THE PRODUCTS

OUR ECONOMY

Goods

Services

£££

Organisations

SPECIALISATION

Production Worker

Accountant

Sales Woman

Examiner's Top Tip
Make a note of real-life examples of specialist firm and people from your own situation.

In our economy, production of goods and services is normally <u>indirect</u>. People don't make goods or produce services for themselves, but instead work with others to provide these products. By doing this, they earn money. The products are then sold in the market-place, people buying them, with money acting as a <u>medium of exchange</u>.

- <u>Firms</u> specialise in their own goods and services, e.g. insurance firms, car manufacturers, banks, DIY stores
- This encourages owners to organise firms into <u>specialist areas</u> such as production, marketing and finance
- As a result, one part of the economy may depend on other parts, for example, specialist manufacturers rely on other specialist firms to insure, advertise and distribute their goods
- <u>People</u> also specialise, by training for specific jobs, e.g. accountants, welders, cashiers, teachers
- This <u>division of labour</u> allows a firm to employ specialists who use specialist machinery and equipment.

EXTERNAL INFLUENCES

Examiner's Top Ti
If you have to explai about 'the governmen remember to include ar relevant EU points.

To sell their products, businesses must have a <u>demand</u> for these goods and services.
- The demand for many goods and services depends on the level of people's <u>incomes</u>.
- Changes occur in people's <u>tastes</u> and <u>fashions</u>.
- The sales of a firm's products will be affected by how successful a <u>competitor's</u> products are.
- The level of demand depends on how well the country's <u>economy</u> is doing.

The success of a business will be influenced by <u>government actions</u>.
- The government creates various <u>laws</u> and <u>regulations</u> that affect business.
- The European Union (EU) and UK government also <u>support</u> firms, e.g. through providing financial assistance and advice.

Nowadays, businesses are heavily influenced by what is happening in our society.
- Greater <u>environmental awareness</u> means that many people are interested in how a firm's activities affect the environment: their buying decisions are influenced by this.
- As a result, firms establish their own <u>ethical policies</u>.

INTERNET

For all the latest on the economy, check out these sites:
www.statistics.gov.uk
www.dti.gov.uk
www.eiu.com
www.economist.co.uk
www.ft.com

THE FACTORS OF PRODUCTION

These four factors of production are the <u>resources</u> that are used to produce the economy's goods and services.

LAND

All businesses need 'land' to create their products. They may:
- actually use the land, e.g. for agriculture, forestry or leisure activities
- build on the land (construction)
- extract raw materials from it, e.g. through mining and quarrying
- rent or buy land for their factories, offices and warehouses.

LABOUR

Businesses need to <u>employ</u> people to make and market their products. The UK's labour force is made up of all the men and women who are available to work.

Product

Examiner's Top Tip
Memorise both the names, and examples of the four factors of production.

CAPITAL

To make their goods or to provide their services, firms need to <u>invest</u> money in machinery, equipment, buildings, vehicles and other major resources. This investment is called 'capital'.

ENTERPRISE

The <u>entrepreneur</u> owns the business and is prepared to take the chance that his or her product will be a success. Entrepreneurs are therefore also known as <u>risk-takers</u>.

Each of these factors receives a <u>financial reward</u>:
- employees earn <u>wages</u>
- the owners of capital receive <u>interest</u>
- entrepreneurs make <u>profits</u>
- the owners of land receive <u>rent</u>.

KEY POINTS

British businesses have three major external influences:
1. the level of demand for their goods and services
2. government policies
3. social and environmental factors.

All economies have to answer three questions:
1. <u>what</u> do we produce?
2. <u>how</u> will this be produced?
3. <u>where</u> will it be produced?

Specialising means that:
- firms can produce their goods and services efficiently
- employees become more efficient at what they do and so may become bored with their work.

QUICK TEST

1. The four factors of production are l_____, l_____, c_____ and e_____
2. What are the main external influences on UK firms?
3. Identify one advantage and one disadvantage from employees specialising.

3. Advantage: employees are more efficient; disadvantage: employees may become bored with their work.
2. Demand for their products; influence of the government; social and environmental factors.
1. Land, labour, capital, enterprise.

TYPES OF ECONOMY

All economies have <u>limited</u> <u>resources</u> and cannot provide all the goods and services that are demanded. As a result, they have to share out – <u>allocate</u> – these resources somehow. There are two main ways used to allocate the resources.

profit

service

DIFFERENT ECONOMIC SYSTEMS

FREE MARKET ECONOMY
- Resources are owned by individuals
- Prices are set through demand and supply
- The profit motive encourages risk-takers (entrepreneurs)

PLANNED ECONOMY
- Resources are owned by the State
- Prices are set by the State
- Supply of goods and services does not depend on the profit motive

Examiner's Top Tip
The price mechanism applies to the factors of production as well as to 'high-street' products.

THE FREE MARKET SYSTEM

Under this system, the working of the <u>price</u> <u>mechanism</u> solves what is produced. Ideally, demand and supply are in <u>equilibrium</u>: the demand for a product matches its supply level.

Where the demand for a product is greater than its supply:
- its price starts to rise
- this cuts the demand
- suppliers who have spare capacity will start making more
- the high price encourages other firms to start supplying the product
- supply will increase to meet the lower demand.

If the supply of a product is greater than its demand:
- its price starts to fall
- this increases its demand
- the lower price discourages some suppliers from selling the product
- supply will fall to meet the higher demand.

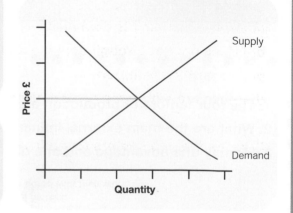

THE PLANNED ECONOMY

Under this system, <u>the State</u> takes control of the economy's resources.

- It establishes <u>price levels</u> for the factors of production and the goods and services supplied.
- It decides <u>what</u> is produced, as well as <u>how</u> and <u>where</u> it is produced.
- In recent years, <u>privatisation</u> has led to many public-sector corporations being transferred to the private sector.
- This has sometimes led to a clash between the objective of <u>providing a service</u> and the objective of <u>making a profit</u>.

KEY POINTS

All economies are part free enterprise and part planned. They are known as <u>mixed economies</u>. The UK's economy has a large <u>private sector</u> providing goods and services through the operation of the price mechanism. The <u>public sector</u> includes national services such as education and health, and local authority organisations.

The strengths of the free market private sector are:
- employers and employees can create their own personal wealth through the profit motive and hard work
- a greater range of products is supplied
- people have greater freedom to choose and buy what they want
- competition helps keep prices down and encourages new ideas.

The strengths of the planned public sector are:
- public services do not depend on the profit motive and will be supplied even at a loss
- the provision of basic services available to all (such as health services), regardless of people's ability to pay for them.

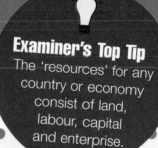

QUICK TEST

1. Which economic system does each point illustrate? Tick the relevant column.

	Free enterprise	Planned
a) Central planning is dominant	☐	☐
b) Prices are set through demand and supply	☐	☐
c) Competition is important	☐	☐
d) Prices are set by the central planning authority	☐	☐

2. Name the two sectors found in a mixed economy.

1. a) Planned b) Free enterprise c) Free enterprise d) Planned
2. Private sector; public sector

LOCATING BUSINESS

INFLUENCES ON WHERE BUSINESSES LOCATE

1. <u>What</u> <u>does</u> <u>it</u> <u>cost</u>? The cost of land varies from region to region.
2. <u>Is</u> <u>there</u> <u>a</u> <u>suitable</u> <u>labour</u> <u>force</u>? People must be able and willing to work where the business is located: if located in an expensive area, the business may have to pay higher wages and salaries.
3. <u>What</u> <u>is</u> <u>the</u> <u>business</u> <u>selling</u>? If it serves a local market, such as a hairdressing or plumbing business, it will locate near its customers; if it has a national market, it is less influenced by where its customers live.
4. <u>Is</u> <u>there</u> <u>government</u> <u>assistance</u>? The EU and the UK government support businesses locating in less well-off regions.
5. <u>What</u> <u>is</u> <u>the</u> <u>infrastructure</u>? The local infrastructure – transport and communications system – must be able to support the business efficiently.
6. <u>Is</u> <u>image</u> <u>relevant</u>? Some locations are valuable for certain types of business, and encourage firms to locate there (e.g. the City of London for a financial institution).

Examiner's Top Tip
Always be prepared to relate the general points about location to real-life business examples.

PEOPLE AND LOCATION

Entrepreneurs will want to ensure that their <u>employees</u> and <u>customers</u> are happy with where the business is located.

<u>Geographical</u> <u>mobility</u> of labour is where <u>workers</u> <u>move</u> <u>to</u> <u>the</u> <u>work</u>. However:
- people may not be willing to move to areas where there is work, e.g. due to family ties
- they may not be able to move because of higher living costs in the areas where there is work.

<u>Occupational</u> <u>mobility</u> of labour occurs where people train or retrain for new jobs
- however, some workers may find they cannot develop the new skills they need.

<u>Customer</u> <u>convenience</u> will influence location:
- in retailing, location near to customers helps small shops survive
- if the business has a more convenient location than its competitors, it will gain at the expense of the competition.

KEY POINTS

Choosing a location is one of the most important business decisions. The decision is heavily influenced by the following factors:
- whether demand for the firm's products is local or national
- the availability of suitable labour
- the cost of land
- government influence
- the personal wishes of the owner(s).

If a firm needs to locate internationally, its owners will take the following factors into account:
- avoiding any <u>trade</u> <u>barriers</u> that may exist
- coping with <u>different</u> <u>cultures</u> <u>and</u> <u>languages</u>
- avoiding countries with a history of <u>political</u> <u>problems</u>.

INTERNET

This will give you more info on business location.

www.dti.gov.uk/regional/index.htm

Examiner's Top Tip
Check businesses near you, and identify the key reasons for the choice of their location.

THE THREE SECTORS

Businesses that need to locate are based in one of three sectors in our economy.

THE PRIMARY SECTOR
- Primary sector businesses <u>extract</u> something: e.g. coal, oil, stone, fish, iron ore.
- The location of these businesses usually depends on where the <u>resources</u> <u>being</u> <u>extracted</u> are found.

THE SECONDARY SECTOR
- Businesses that <u>construct</u> or <u>manufacture</u> something are in this sector.
- Their location is influenced by many factors, such as <u>government</u> <u>support</u> and the existence of a <u>suitable</u> <u>labour</u> <u>force</u>.

THE TERTIARY SECTOR
- This '<u>service</u>' sector supports the other two sectors. Services include transport, finance, insurance, training and advertising.
- Their location will be influenced by the services required by firms in the other two sectors.

Examiner's Top Tip
The tertiary sector has recently become even more important in the UK economy.

QUICK TEST

1. Classify each of these businesses as either primary, secondary or tertiary:

   a) a specialist distribution firm

   b) a builder

   c) a building society

   d) a forestry plantation

   e) a computer manufacturer

2. List four major influences on location.

1. d) primary, b) and e) secondary, a) and c) tertiary.
2. Cost; availability of labour; nature of the product; influence of the government.

THE EUROPEAN UNION

Examiner's Top Tip
Although you don't need to study the EMU in great detail, it's useful to know the main arguments.

IMPORTANCE OF THE UNION

The European Union contains four of the world's major economic powers: France, Germany, Italy and the United Kingdom. The EU is now the UK's main market.

Examiner's Top Tip
Make sure you know that the EU assists, and also helps control, firms in the UK.

UK IMPORTS IN 2000

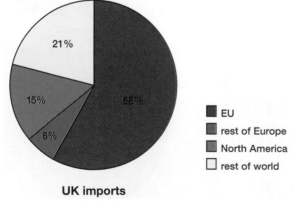

21%
15%
6%
58%

- EU
- rest of Europe
- North America
- rest of world

UK imports

UK EXPORTS IN 2000

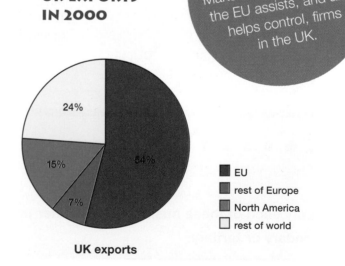

24%
15%
7%
54%

- EU
- rest of Europe
- North America
- rest of world

UK exports

Many of the UK's laws are based on EU <u>Directives</u> and <u>Regulations</u>. The EU's influence includes:
- supporting equal treatment in the workplace
- protecting employees from exploitation
- encouraging greater industrial democracy by getting workers more involved in decision-making.

The EU's <u>Social Charter</u> protects the rights of workers, and covers areas of work such as working hours, the right to join a union, and health and safety.

THE SINGLE MARKET

Promoting trade between the member states was a major influence in establishing the EU. Its 'Common Market' is now a single market consisting of about 400 million people.

The main purposes of the Single Market are to establish:
- free movement of <u>people</u> (labour)
- free movement of <u>goods</u> (no internal tariffs)
- common technical and other <u>standards</u>.

Examples of single market activity include:
- <u>CE marking</u> – if a product is to be sold or used within the EU it must carry the <u>CE mark</u> which indicates that the product has met with essential health and safety requirements set by the EU.
- <u>competition policy</u> and <u>merger control regulations</u> – to control monopolies in member states so free and fair trade can take place
- <u>consumer protection</u> – including guaranteed information about prices and e-commerce providers, and protection against unfair advertising and unsafe products.

The Single Market has influenced UK business in several ways:
- common standards of quality and safety have been set throughout the EU, which UK firms must meet
- open markets encourage competition, requiring UK firms to be efficient in order to compete successfully
- free movement of labour and goods encourages employment and skill development.

MONETARY UNION

Most of the EU's member states are in the <u>Eurozone</u>, having agreed to adopt the euro as their future currency. The UK did not join the Eurozone in 1999. From 2002, transactions in the Eurozone's financial markets will be carried out in euros. Households will also use the euro as their currency.

<u>Economic</u> and <u>Monetary Union</u> (EMU) is closely linked with the euro and Eurozone. The single currency will affect the EU:
- since trade will be valued in euros, <u>exchange rate fluctuations</u> between different currencies will no longer happen – this makes trade between these member states much easier, and there will be no need to change national currencies
- <u>price differences</u> between member states will be much easier to see, as a result of the single currency.

The UK businesses most affected by EMU are <u>importers</u> and <u>exporters</u>, and UK-based <u>multinationals</u> and <u>financial institutions</u>. These and other UK firms will need to consider how the euro and the Eurozone affects:
- their <u>competition</u>
- how they <u>price</u> their goods and services.

QUICK TEST

1. In the EU, what is the Social Charter?
2. What is the difference between the Eurozone and the euro?
3. What does the EU's Single Market seek to do?

INTERNATIONAL BUSINESS

WHY DO WE TRADE INTERNATIONALLY?

The United Kingdom relies on trade for the following reasons:
- the UK economy does not try to provide all the goods demanded by its population
- like all advanced economies, our economy specialises in providing certain goods and services
- we therefore create surpluses, which we trade with other countries
- some raw materials do not exist in the UK and so have to be imported
- certain goods cannot be produced in the UK, e.g. because of its climate.

BENEFITS FOR BUSINESS

Export markets provide a number of opportunities for UK business.

1. Sales increase
- by exporting, businesses have a bigger market in which to sell their products
- these markets are newer, and less saturated with their products than the UK market.

2. Economies of scale become possible
- as sales increase, the business gains from certain economies, e.g. being able to bulk-buy its raw materials at ower prices, or through using specialist machinery

- as a result, its lower unit costs make it more price-competitive.

3. Spreading the risk
- through trading in different markets, the business is not relying on a single market.
- it can expand its operations in other markets if one of its markets becomes difficult to trade in.

Businesses also gain from importing.

a) Lower costs
- the business may discover that it can obtain its supplies more cheaply from abroad
- these items may also be of better quality, and therefore better value for money, than those sold in the home market.

b) Greater choice
- businesses buying and selling directly to consumers (e.g. retailers) will improve their product mix from selling both home-produced and imported goods
- by doing so, they offer their customers greater choice.

PROBLEMS FOR BUSINESSES

Both exporting and importing present a business with problems to overcome.

COSTS AND PRICES
- When trading overseas, the business has to cope with <u>exchange rate</u> <u>fluctuations</u> in the prices of the foreign currencies in which it must deal.
- This even applies in the Single Market, because <u>the UK is not part of the Eurozone</u>.
- These currency price changes make it <u>difficult for UK businesses to work out costs and set prices</u>.

DIFFERENT CULTURE AND LANGUAGE
- Since overseas markets consist of people with different cultures, UK exporters will need to be aware of the <u>different likes and dislikes</u> of these cultures.
- Different languages also mean the business must <u>change how it markets</u> its products, e.g. re-labelling them in these other languages.
- <u>Communication</u> becomes more difficult with the overseas markets.

COMPETITION FROM OVERSEAS
- UK-based firms face stiff <u>competition from businesses</u> originally based in the overseas market, as well as from <u>other exporters</u> to that market.
- Overseas firms also compete in the UK economy.

TRADE BARRIERS
- The UK exporter may have to pay <u>tariffs</u> (import duties), a type of tax that raises the price of the item and makes it less competitive.
- <u>Quotas</u> – physical restrictions on the numbers of goods – may also affect the ability of a UK business to export to a particular overseas market.

Examiner's Top Tip
You should acknowledge that the UK is in the Single Market when answering questions on international trade.

RECORDING TRADE

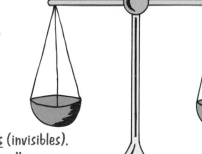

INTERNET

www.tradepartners.gov.uk

The UK's balance of payments (1998)

Current account (£m)	
Trade in goods	– 20 765
Trade in services	12 253
Total trade	– 8 512
Other adjustments	8 648
Current balance	136

International investment (£m)	
Investment abroad	110.6
Investment in the UK	– 95.5
Net earnings	15.1

- The <u>balance of trade</u> measures the UK's <u>visible</u> imports and exports.
- The <u>Current account</u> records trade in these goods, and also trade in <u>services</u> (invisibles).
- The <u>Capital account</u> shows the effect of <u>buying and selling assets internationally</u>.

QUICK TEST

1. What are the benefits for consumers from international trade?

2. For a UK-based firm, in what ways is trade in the Single Market a) similar to, and b) different from, trade outside the EU?

1. Greater choice; lower prices through greater competition.
2. a) problems of different cultures and language; extra have to be met; competition from EU-based and other firms; exchange rate difficulties.
b) a single market with similar requirements for products (e.g. safety); paperwork and other administrative requirements are the same throughout the EU.

UNINCORPORATED

Both sole traders and partnerships are examples of unincorporated businesses. There are two major results of being 'unincorporated'.

UNLIMITED LIABILITY
- The owners have unlimited liability for their business debts.
- If necessary, they may be forced to <u>use their personal wealth to settle business debts</u>.

LEGAL EXISTENCE
- In law, the sole trader's business or the partners' business <u>does not have a separate legal existence</u>.
- This means that legal action is taken by or against the individual sole trader or partner, rather than in the name of the business.
- As a result, business contracts are entered into by the owners rather than by the business.
- Because it does not have a separate legal existence, <u>a change in ownership can end the business</u>.

SOLE TRADER AND PARTNERSHIP BUSINESSES

SOLE TRADERS

The sole trader remains the UK's most popular form of business. This business <u>is owned by a single individual</u>, although any number of people may be employed in the business by the owner.

ADVANTAGES
- A small-scale business such as a sole trader only needs a relatively <u>small amount of capital</u>.
- The owner <u>does not have to share profits</u> with others.
- The owner is 'the boss'.
- It is <u>quick and simple to set up</u> in business as a sole trader, although the owner must <u>register the business for tax purposes</u>.
- <u>Quick decisions</u> can be made, the owner being able to respond swiftly to market changes.

DISADVANTAGES
- <u>Unlimited liability</u> is the main drawback.
- Since there is no separate legal existence, <u>the business does not automatically continue</u> after the owner finishes.
- The small-scale nature of the business makes it <u>difficult to obtain capital</u> for expansion.
- 'The boss' has <u>all the responsibility</u>, and may have to work long hours.

Examiner's Top Tip
Identify real-life examples you can quote in answers.

Examiner's Top Tip
You are often tested on the advantages and disadvantages of these business forms.

PARTNERSHIPS

Examiner's Top Tip
You may be asked to analyse the benefits of changing from a sole trader to a partnership.

These businesses can also be formed easily. The partners normally draw up a <u>partnership</u> <u>agreement</u> to record:

· how <u>profits</u> and <u>losses</u> <u>will be shared</u>
· the amount of <u>capital</u> <u>invested</u> <u>by</u> <u>each partner</u>
· individual <u>rights</u> (e.g. to a salary) and work <u>responsibilities</u>.

Compared with sole traders:

· partners can <u>share</u> <u>decision-making</u>, although this can lead to <u>disputes</u> between the partners
· responsibility can be shared, allowing individual partners more free time
· partners can <u>specialise</u> in different business functions
· <u>more</u> <u>capital</u> can usually be invested and obtained by the partnership, although there is a legal limit of 20 partners in an ordinary partnership
· 'sleeping' <u>partners</u> may supply capital but will take no part in running the business.

The <u>limited</u> <u>liability</u> <u>partnership</u> (LLP) is a new form of partnership. The partnership is still <u>easy</u> <u>to</u> <u>establish</u> and its members gain from <u>limited</u> <u>liability</u>. They <u>must</u> <u>draw</u> <u>up</u> <u>a</u> <u>members'</u> <u>agreement</u> (similar to a partnership agreement).

INTERNET

All the information you need on those who go it alone!
www.businessadviceonline.org.uk

KEY POINTS

- Remember that sole traders and partners usually work in businesses <u>with</u> <u>limited or</u> <u>local</u> <u>demand</u>.
- Popular examples of sole traders include the 'corner shop', and small high-street businesses such as florists and hairdressers.
- Other service-based sole traders include craftspeople such as plumbers and electricians.
- Specialist firms such as antique shops often operate as sole traders.
- Partnerships are commonly found in the 'professions', such as doctors, accountants and lawyers.
- In practice, <u>franchising</u> is an increasingly popular form of business, similar in many ways to a sole trader.

QUICK TEST

1. The two main features of being unincorporated are u_____ l_____
   and no s_____ l_____ e_____.
2. What is the maximum number of people who can a) own, and b) work in, a sole trader business?
3. Find at least two examples of a) sole trader and b) partnership businesses in your local area.

1. Unlimited liability; separate legal existence.
2. a) one; b) there is no legal maximum.

INCORPORATED

Unlike sole traders and partnerships, a limited company is an **incorporated** **business**. As a result:

- the company has a **separate** **legal** **existence** from that of its owners (**shareholders**)
- legal action will be taken in the name of the limited company, rather than in the name of the shareholders
- shareholders (and other people) can sue the company
- this separate legal existence also means the company has **greater** **continuity**, because its existence is not ended by the death or retirement of its shareholders
- the owners have **limited** **liability** for their business debts
- the owners cannot be made to use their own wealth to settle any business debts.

An important benefit from limited liability is that the shareholders know exactly how much money they risk losing. This **encourages** **people** **to** **invest**, knowing there is a limit to the amount they can lose.

PRIVATE AND PUBLIC

Private limited companies must include the word limited in their name, and public companies the words public limited company. The abbreviations ltd and plc are widely used.

ADVANTAGES OF BEING PRIVATE	ADVANTAGES OF BEING PUBLIC
• Private companies can keep their business affairs more private than PLCs, because members of the public (and therefore competitors) do not have access to their accounts. • Private companies are less likely than PLCs to suffer from bureaucracy ('red tape') and from diseconomies of scale (their unit costs start to rise). • Compared with PLCs, ownership of a private company is not so subject to hostile takeover bids because its shares can not be bought on the Stock Exchange.	• PLCs can raise capital from members of the public, unlike private companies. • PLCs are usually larger than private companies, and therefore gain from economies of scale. • PLCs are more likely to be able to employ specialists, and to use specialist machinery and equipment. • Through their greater size and their ability to ask the public to buy shares, PLCs find it easier to obtain capital.

INTERNET

Some useful sites:
www.kellys.co.uk
www.bigstoresuk.co.uk
www.britishcompanies.co.uk
www.ukpages.co.uk

COMPANY DOCUMENTS

- The **memorandum of association** outlines the company's **external** relationship; it states the company's name and its purpose, and where its registered office is located.
- The **articles of association** document records the company's internal workings, e.g. of directors and their election.
- The company will also publish its **final accounts**: the PLC's accounts can be obtained by members of the public.

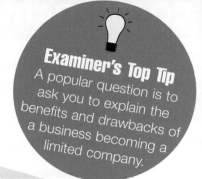

Examiner's Top Tip
A popular question is to ask you to explain the benefits and drawbacks of a business becoming a limited company.

Glaxo SmithKline   Sony Corporation   *Ford*   Mitsubishi Electric Corporation

LIMITED COMPANIES

Tesco   Somerfield   *hp*   Pizza Express   Marks & Spencer

OWNERSHIP VERSUS CONTROL

Limited companies face a <u>separation of ownership from control</u>.
- The company's <u>shareholders</u> tend to have little say in the daily running of the company.
- It is the company's <u>directors</u> who control the company.
- These directors are elected by the shareholders at the company's <u>annual general meeting</u> (AGM).
- The board of directors establishes overall policy, and delegates to managers some of the responsibility for achieving the company's objectives.
- The shareholders and directors may have <u>different views</u> and objectives, different opinions on the speed of the company's growth and the levels of its profit.

QUICK TEST

1. State two differences between private and public limited companies.
2. Why is the separation of ownership from control important?
3. Identify two differences between incorporated and unincorporated businesses.

3. Incorporated businesses can take and defend legal actions in their own name; incorporated businesses have limited liability.
2. Shareholders (owners) may wish the company to follow different policies from those the directors (controllers) want.
1. Private companies cannot sell their shares to the public; private company accounts are not available to the public.

CO-OPERATIVES

- Producer (or worker) co-operatives are created when people join together to provide a product. In the UK, some worker co-operatives were created by employees buying out their company because it was in financial difficulties.
- Retail co-operatives are created when consumers join together to buy in bulk.
- Individual retail co-operatives are supplied by the CWS, the Co-operative Wholesale Society.

OTHER BUSINESSES

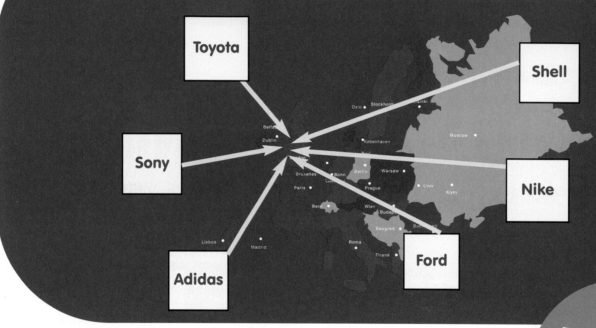

MULTINATIONALS

A **multinational** is an organisation with its headquarters in one country, and which carries out operations in other countries. In the UK, multinationals are normally PLCs.

Multinationals have developed because:
- they can gain from low-cost labour and other factors of production – e.g. producing in low-wage countries cuts production costs and makes the multinational's products more price-competitive
- they can sometimes avoid trade barriers – e.g. many multinationals have set up business in the UK and other EU countries in order to avoid paying the Single Market's common external tariff
- they are able to spread risk by diversifying into different countries' markets.

Multinationals support the UK economy through:
- providing jobs, which helps to reduce unemployment
- bringing in new expertise and new technology
- bringing in new ideas (e.g. successful work practices from the Far East).

The drawbacks of multinationals operating in an economy are:
- they are in a strong bargaining position and can influence the government's policies
- different work practices can lead to disputes
- they may export their profits.

Examiner's Top Tip
Points for and against both multinationals and public ownership are often tested.

FRANCHISES

A franchise is created when a person goes into business to sell a named product supplied by a major supplier. The person taking out the franchise – the <u>franchisee</u> – supplies the capital, and in return receives training, the product, marketing expertise and general support from the <u>franchisor</u>. Examples of franchising companies include McDonald's and other major 'fast-food' chains, and The Body Shop.

- <u>Advantages</u> <u>to</u> <u>the</u> <u>franchisee</u> – gaining a well-known product, trading name and reputation, and receiving the franchisor's expert support.
- <u>Advantages to the franchisor</u> – gaining outlets without having to find the capital to finance them, and a willing franchisee who is likely to work hard to make a success of the franchise.

Examiner's Top Tip
You may be asked to compare franchises with traditional sole traders as forms of ownership.

PUBLIC CORPORATIONS AND LOCAL AUTHORITY BUSINESSES

<u>Public</u> <u>corporations</u> are what we used to call <u>nationalised</u> <u>industries</u>. These organisations are <u>owned</u> <u>by</u> <u>the</u> <u>State</u>, and supply goods and services to the whole economy.

- The Conservative governments of the 1980s <u>privatised</u> many public corporations on the grounds that these industries were inefficient, suffered from diseconomies of scale, and would therefore be <u>more</u> <u>efficient</u> under private ownership.

Arguments in favour of public ownership are:
- it is a way of <u>controlling</u> <u>natural</u> <u>monopolies</u>
- it guarantees that <u>essential</u> <u>services</u> will be provided
- certain areas of the economy (e.g. defence) need to be controlled centrally because of <u>national</u> <u>security</u>.

Many <u>local</u> <u>authorities</u> operate businesses such as sports centres, or use land to obtain revenue (e.g. from car parking charges). These may be <u>profit-making</u> <u>activities</u>, which provide revenue for the local authority.

Examiner's Top Tip
Learn the definition of a multinational.

QUICK TEST

1. List two benefits and two drawbacks to a country from having multinationals in its economy.
2. The organisation creating the franchise is the f_____ , and people who buy franchises from it are the f_____.
3. What are the two main forms of co-operative?

3. Retail; producer (worker).
2. Franchisor; franchisees.
1. Benefits: the multinational provides jobs, and brings in new ideas. Drawbacks: it is in a powerful position, and it can export its profits to its home country.

BUSINESS OBJECTIVES

PRIVATE SECTOR businesses are owned by individuals, who may have a number of different objectives. These objectives are set by the entrepreneurs, and often include:

- survival – the owners will want the business to survive, and may therefore put up with losses in the short term
- profit – a profit target will be set, so that the owners receive some of this as a reward for risking investing their money, and can use the profits made to measure the success of the business
- growth – by growing in size, larger organisations find it easier to survive, e.g. by diversifying (selling different products in different markets) and through gaining economies of scale
- market share – the larger the share of the market, the more dominant the firm can be, e.g. by setting price levels.

PUBLIC SECTOR organisations are owned by the State, whose officials (e.g. politicians) set the objectives for these businesses. The objectives may be more to do with providing an efficient service than with making profits.

STAKEHOLDERS IN BUSINESS

INTERNAL STAKEHOLDERS

ENTREPRENEURS

Entrepreneurs are particularly interested in their firm's survival, and the likelihood of profits. This profit motive may clash with the objectives of other stakeholder groups. For example:

- customers want low prices, which cut profit margins
- employees want high pay and job security, which may conflict with the push for profits
- lenders and suppliers are more interested in the organisation's liquidity – its ability to pay the debts owed to them.

EMPLOYEES

All employees will wish to see the business be successful, to keep their jobs and income. They may also benefit through share ownership or profit-sharing schemes.

- The performance of the employees is a key factor in the success of the business.
- Owners and managers are usually keen to consult with the employees about their work and feelings.

Examiner's Top Tip
Remember to explain that different stakeholders will have different objectives.

SHAREHOLDERS

As the <u>owners</u> of limited companies, shareholders have an interest in the company's <u>financial</u> <u>performance</u>. In some companies, especially the private limited type, the main shareholders are also directors or managers, and therefore internal to the company.

- Although ordinary shareholders own the profits of the company, it is the directors who decide how much profit will be distributed to the ordinary shareholders.
- The directors' policies on distributing profits, and on other issues (e.g. environmental matters), can sometimes lead to disputes between those who <u>own</u> and those who <u>control</u> the company.

Examiner's Top Tip
It can be helpful to group stakeholders as internal and external.

CUSTOMERS

Customers have opinions on how the business operates.

- They sometimes join together to act as a <u>consumer</u> <u>pressure</u> <u>group</u>.
- If they are unhappy with the firm's work, or with the quality of its products, they will stop being customers.

EXTERNAL STAKEHOLDERS

SUPPLIERS

Suppliers are stakeholders in the business, because if it fails, they will lose a customer and therefore lose sales.

LENDERS

Lenders are stakeholders, for the following reasons.

- They have invested money in the business.
- They expect to receive a return on their investment (e.g. interest payments).
- They want their money back in future.

THE COMMUNITY

The local population are also stakeholders. They are particularly interested in the organisation's:

- <u>employment</u> policy – it is a source of work for them
- <u>environmental</u> policy – its work affects their quality of life.

The organisation may create <u>positive</u> <u>externalities</u>, such as better local roads and transport, but it can also create <u>negative</u> <u>externalities</u> such as pollution.

Examiner's Top Tip
Identify real-life stakeholders for those organisations you have studied.

QUICK TEST

1. What is a 'stakeholder'?

2. For each stakeholder group, suggest one area of interest in the firm's work:

   a) Shareholders

   b) Directors

   c) Employees

   d) Customers

   e) Local community

   f) Lenders

1. A person (or group of people) having a direct interest in an organisation's work and performance.
2. a) profit level; b) survival of the business; c) job security; d) quality of product; e) effect on the local environment; f) liquidity (can the business meet its debts?)

EXAM QUESTIONS — Use the questions to test your progress. Check your answers on page 94.

1. List **three** examples of industries in the secondary sector.

....

2. Which of the following is a factor of production?
a) Supply ☐
b) Franchise ☐
c) Profit ☐
d) Labour ☐

3. Tick the phrase that best explains the term 'limited liability':

The business is limited to the products it is allowed to make ☐
The owners are limited to the amount they can lose in the business ☐
The number of meetings that can be held is limited ☐
The business has a maximum number of 20 owners ☐
The amount of capital that can be invested is limited ☐
Employees are limited as to what they can do in the business ☐

4. The following features are associated with either a sole trader, a partnership, or one of the types of limited company. For each, identify the most appropriate form of business ownership:
a) The owners usually create a written agreement

....
....

b) All profits go to the owner, who also bears all the losses

....

c) There are typically from 2 to 20 owners

....

d) Economies of scale are most likely

....

e) Shares can be issued, but not advertised for sale to the public at large

....

5. Explain briefly how the price mechanism operates.

....
....

6. Oakworth Ltd makes garden sheds and other wooden products. It originally started as a partnership, but the owners converted it to a private limited company. As the business has continued to grow, one owner has suggested turning it into a PLC.
a) Give **two** reasons why the owners might have decided to change the business to a limited company.

....
....

b) Why might the other owner of Oakworth Ltd want to keep it as a private company?

....
....

7. In December 2000 Jim Bentley was made redundant. He wanted to use the redundancy money to buy a small shop. Jim has been offered a franchise with a major petrol supplier. He now runs a garage and forecourt shop.

a) What names are given to:

i) a person like Jim who invests in a franchise?

....

ii) the companies that sell franchises?

....

b) Suggest **two** advantages and **two** disadvantages to Jim in entering into a franchise rather than becoming a traditional sole trader

....

....

c) Identify **two** business objectives Jim is likely to have ....

....

d) How might these objectives differ from those of the petrol company? ....

....

8. Putitin Ltd makes metal containers that it sells to other businesses. The company is located in the Midlands. The directors are investigating whether the company can start exporting to the rest of the EU. If they decide to export, they will consider relocating the business to south-east England.

a) In which sector of production, and in which sector of the economy, is Putitin Ltd based?

....

....

b) i) Identify **two** stakeholder groups this company will have.

....

....

ii) For each group, explain why it is interested in the company's performance.

....

....

c) What benefits and problems might Putitin Ltd face if it starts trading with the rest of the EU?

....

....

d) Explain how exporting to the rest of the EU will differ from exporting to non-EU countries in Europe.

....

....

e) Explain **four** factors that the directors will consider when taking the decision to relocate.

....

....

....

....

How did you do?

1–2	correct	start again
3–4	correct	getting there
5–6	correct	good work
7–8	correct	excellent

PRODUCTION OF GOODS AND SERVICES

Lean production can overcome some of mass production's drawbacks, e.g. by using capacity and improving morale.
'Just-in-time' reduces the costs of stockholding, but any delivery problem can halt all production.

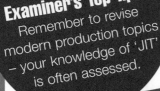

Examiner's Top Tip
Remember to revise modern production topics – your knowledge of 'JIT' is often assessed.

30p each or 4 for £1

<u>Job</u> production occurs where a single product is made to customer requirements.
<u>Batch production</u> involves making similar items in set numbers ('batches').
<u>Mass production</u> creates large numbers of identical, standardised products.
Mass (continuous) production often leads to <u>economies</u> <u>of</u> <u>scale</u> – these include managerial, purchasing, financial, marketing, technical and risk-bearing.

PRODUCTS

THE MAIN FUNCTIONS OF

PEOPLE

PEOPLE: HUMAN RESOURCE MANAGEMENT (HRM)

EMPLOYING

JOB DESCRIPTION **Details of the job**	PERSON SPECIFICATION: **Details of the person**
job title hours pay	skills qualifications

- **Recruiting** – *either internally or externally*

- **Selecting** – *interviews, aptitude and other tests*

- **Appointing** – *issuing the contract of employment*

- **Inducting**

TRAINING

After induction training, the firm will offer more training, either <u>internal</u> or <u>external</u>.

On-the-job internal training is specific to the firm, but may be delivered by non-specialists.

Off-the-job external training is delivered by trained staff, but is not exclusively for the firm.

Other functions of the HRM (personnel) department include:

- *negotiating with trade unions and other employee associations*
- *paying wages and salaries.*

HRM therefore deals with people who are working or who wish to work for the firm.

FINANCE: THE ACCOUNTING FUNCTION

LOOKING FORWARDS
<u>Budgets</u> plan for the future and set performance targets.
* Cash budgeting helps to ensure <u>liquidity</u>.
* Fixed and variable costs are analysed to calculate the firm's <u>break-even point</u>.

LOOKING BACK
Financial accounting:
* <u>records</u> financial transactions
* <u>calculates</u> the firm's profit or loss
* <u>displays</u> the firm's assets and liabilities
* <u>assesses</u> the firm's performance (through accounting ratios).

OBTAINING FINANCE
This is a key role. The finance may come from:
* <u>internal sources</u> – personal savings or retained profits.
* <u>external sources</u> – <u>long-term capital</u> such as shares and debentures, and <u>short-term capital</u> e.g. trade credit, bank overdraft.

POUNDS & PENCE

BUSINESS

PROMOTING SALES

MARKETING: PROMOTING AND SELLING

A product's market can often be broken down into different <u>segments</u> – e.g. by age and income. <u>Market research</u> is necessary to provide information about the firm's 'marketing mix'. This 'mix' consists of:

PRODUCT: Product <u>differentiation</u> is important. Firms also analyse product <u>lifecycles</u>.

PRICE: <u>High price</u> strategies include skimming, maximising and premium pricing. <u>Low-price</u> ones include penetration and capturing.

PLACE: The product will need to be distributed through <u>channels</u> – e.g. by wholesalers to retailers.

PROMOTION: The four main methods are <u>advertising</u>, <u>sales promotion</u>, <u>direct marketing</u> and <u>personal selling</u>. The Internet has increased in importance as an advertising/promotion medium.

> **Examiner's Top Tip**
> Learn the main profitability and liquidity ratios. (see page 58).

QUICK TEST

1. Name three economies of scale.
2. Why do firms carry out cash budgeting?
3. What is the difference between a job description and a person specification?
4. State the four main methods of promotion.

> **Examiner's Top Tip**
> Check the Internet for business pages, e.g. how Tesco and Iceland sell using the Web.

1. Technical, marketing, risk-bearing. 2. To make sure they have enough cash in the future. 3. The job description gives details of the job, person specification gives details of the person. 4. Advertising, sales promotion, direct marketing, personal selling.

ORGANISING BUSINESS

- There will be a close link between a firm's <u>objectives</u> and the way it is organised (its <u>structure</u>): most private sector firms are organised by <u>function</u>, whereas central and local government organisations are normally organised by the <u>service</u> they offer.
- Organisation allows <u>specialisation</u> to take place, which can lead to greater <u>efficiency</u>.

ORGANISATIONAL TERMS

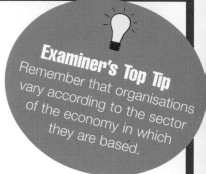

An organisation will have a <u>hierarchy</u>, shown by its organisation chart. The <u>status</u> of employees in the hierarchy is shown by the <u>chain</u> of <u>command</u>, which runs from the directors to the managers, then through the departments to the shop floor and office workers.

Managers need to <u>delegate</u> some decisions and tasks to their staff (their <u>subordinates</u>). This delegation flows down the chain of command.

When delegating, the manager must give the member of staff the <u>authority</u> to make the decision and to do the task. By doing so, the employee now has the <u>responsibility</u> to do the work, and becomes <u>accountable</u> to the manager.

Where a lot of delegation exists, the firm is likely to have a <u>decentralised</u> structure: little delegation is associated with a more <u>centralised</u> structure.

The manager will need to <u>supervise, co-ordinate</u> and <u>control</u> the work being done by the employees. The number of staff under an individual manager's control indicates that manager's <u>span</u> of <u>control</u>.

TALL AND FLAT STRUCTURES
A firm's structure may be tall or flat. This indicates the <u>number</u> of <u>levels</u> found in the firm's hierarchy.
A <u>tall</u> structure is associated with:
- long chains of command
- narrow spans of control
- specialised staff
- slower decision-making
- formal communication systems.

As a result, many firms have tried to <u>flatten</u> their structures, to speed up communication and cut out <u>bureaucracy</u> (red tape). This is known as <u>delayering</u>.

ORGANISATION BY FUNCTION

Examiner's Top Tip
It's helpful to study how real firms are organised.

This form of organisation relates to a <u>role</u> culture, with clearly defined job descriptions, chains of command and lines of communication.

- **The role of the organisation chart is to show the firm's <u>internal</u> <u>structure</u>.**
- **It shows chains of command as a series of lines, illustrating the <u>line</u> <u>authority</u> of departmental managers.**
- **The chart can become out-of-date.**
- **It will not show the <u>informal</u> <u>communication</u> and other informal links that will exist in the firm.**
- **It is not always easy to show on the chart those employees who have a <u>specialist</u> <u>staff</u> function.**

ORGANISATION BY TASK

Examiner's Top Tip
Study the 'language' of organisation: there are many important words and terms used.

	purchasing manager	production manager	sales manager
manager 'standard' model	□	□	□
manager 'super' model	□	□	□
manager 'super-duper' model	□	□	□

- One effect of 'flattening' an organisation's structure is that emphasis may move from the traditional department towards a more <u>task-based</u> structure.
- This is sometimes called a <u>matrix</u> structure.
- Although traditional departments may still exist, staff from different departments work together on set tasks and projects.
- Matrix organisation often exists in flatter structures, where managers have wide spans of control.

QUICK TEST

1. What is the difference between 'span of control' and 'chain of command'?
2. Why have many firms attempted to 'flatten' their organisational structure?
3. Draw the organisation chart for a business you have studied.

1. Span of control is the number of staff under a manager/supervisor; chain of command is how the hierarchy is organised.
2. To improve communication and decision-making, and to reduce the feeling of 'distance' between those at the top and those at the bottom of the hierarchy.

COMMUNICATING IN BUSINESS

FORMS OF COMMUNICATION

There are many groups with whom the organisation must communicate. These include:
- _internal_ groups, such as managers, employees, union representatives
- _external_ groups, e.g. shareholders, suppliers, lenders, customers.

In every case, the communication should be as _quick_ as is required, as _clear_ as possible, and as _detailed_ as necessary.

ORAL COMMUNICATION
- _Meetings_ are (usually) formal settings for oral communication.
- The _telephone_ is often the main method of communicating orally with suppliers.
- Oral communication tends to be _quicker_ than written forms, and allows _interpretation_ and _further discussion_.
- It _lacks the permanent nature_ of written communication: it cannot easily be stored and referred to later.

WRITTEN COMMUNICATION
- _Letters_ are sent mainly externally as formal communication, whereas _memos_ tend to be used internally for more informal communication.
- _Email_ is an increasingly popular way of sending memos and letters electronically, often being preferred to fax.
- Company _magazines_ and _notices_ are sometimes transmitted as email attachments.
- The organisation's _annual report and accounts_ will be sent in written form to shareholders.
- _Reports_ are written on major areas of development or concern, e.g. progress of a new product.
- A written record of meetings is kept as _minutes_, and the _agenda_ will also be in written form.

VISUAL COMMUNICATION
- This form of communication is used to _simplify_ and _summarise_ words and numbers.
- Organisations use _pictures_, _charts_, _graphs_ and other forms of visual display.

elements of price

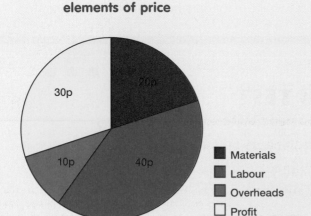

- Materials
- Labour
- Overheads
- Profit

sales performance

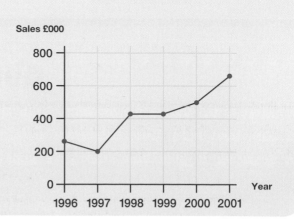

COMMUNICATION THEORY

Examiner's Top Tip
Study how firms communicate using papers, the TV and the Internet.

The key elements in using communication are: the <u>transmitter</u> (sender of the message); the <u>recipient</u> (receiver of the message); the <u>message</u> itself; and the <u>medium</u> by which the message is being sent. In business, all these elements must function effectively for communication to be efficient.

Good communication is influenced by:
- the <u>attitudes</u> of the sender and receiver
- their <u>knowledge</u> of the subject – matter being communicated
- <u>what</u> is being communicated – sending instructions, giving advice, asking for opinions or presenting facts
- <u>how</u> it is being communicated – the <u>suitability</u> of the communication medium used
- the amount of <u>noise</u> present (anything that affects the message being transmitted and received clearly and accurately).

The main barriers to communication include <u>complex</u> <u>language</u>, <u>unsuitable</u> <u>medium</u>, <u>over-long</u> <u>message</u>, and <u>bias</u> on the part of the sender or receiver.

COMMUNICATION IN TRADING

There will be a flow of trading documents between <u>buyer</u> and <u>seller</u>.

B U Y E R → letter of enquiry →
← quotation, catalogue and price list ←
→ order →
← advice note ←
← delivery note ←
← invoice ←
← statement of account ←
→ payment (e.g. cheque) → **S E L L E R**

The <u>invoice</u> is the main trading document. It contains:
- **details of the goods ordered**
- **information on delivery**
- **any VAT and settlement discount being offered.**

Examiner's Top Tip
Remember communication may have to be stored, retrieved and transmitted.

QUICK TEST

1. With which major groups will an organisation need to communicate?
2. What influences how the organisation communicates its information?
3. What are the main causes of poor communication?

1. Internal: managers, employes. External: shareholders, customers, suppliers, lenders, government.
2. Degree of formality required; whether permanent communication record is needed; volume of information; speed necessary; nature of information (e.g. whether technical or not).
3. Length of message; over-complex language used; 'noise'; missing out key information.

HOW A BUSINESS GROWS

INTEGRATION

In a <u>merger</u> two companies agree to join.

This <u>external</u> growth is the quickest way for organisations to grow.

In a <u>takeover</u> one company buys enough of another company's voting shares to take control.

THREE FORMS OF INTEGRATION

<u>HORIZONTAL</u>: between companies in the <u>same</u> <u>industry</u> and at the <u>same</u> <u>stage</u> of production. This integration <u>increases</u> <u>market</u> <u>share</u> <u>and</u> <u>power</u>, and leads to <u>economies</u> <u>of scale</u>.

<u>VERTICAL</u>: between companies in the <u>same</u> <u>industry</u> but at <u>different</u> <u>stages</u> of production. This form of integration <u>strengthens</u> <u>control</u> <u>over</u> <u>supply</u> <u>and</u> <u>sales</u> <u>of the</u> <u>products</u>.
- Vertical <u>backwards</u> is when the company controls firms back down the chain of production.
- Vertical <u>forwards</u> is when the company controls firms closer to the final customer.

<u>LATERAL</u> (<u>conglomerate</u>): between companies in <u>different</u> <u>industries</u>. This integration helps the company <u>diversify</u> into different markets, which <u>reduces</u> <u>risk</u>. If one market fails, the company can continue trading in its other market(s).

MEASURING SIZE

Several methods are used to measure an organisation's size: there is no best method.

<u>profits</u>
how much the business keeps from selling its goods/services

<u>turnover</u>
the sales that the business makes

<u>employees</u>
the number of people employed in the business

<u>capital</u> <u>employed</u>
the resources the business has invested in it

Examiner's Top Tip
This topic links closely to economies of scale: study them together.

KEY POINTS

For a firm, greater size through growth makes:
- <u>economies</u> <u>of</u> <u>scale</u> possible
- <u>survival</u> more likely.

Organisations can grow <u>organically</u> (internally) as well as through mergers or takeovers. This internal form of growth happens when an organisation:

- <u>sells</u> <u>more</u> of its existing products
- starts selling <u>new</u> <u>products</u>
- enters <u>new</u> <u>markets</u>.

QUICK TEST

1. Distinguish between:
   a) internal and external growth
   b) mergers and takeovers
   c) horizontal, vertical and lateral growth.
2. State two benefits arising from growth.

Examiner's Top Tip
You will probably have to explain why size and growth are important to organisations.

1.a) Internal: growth within the organisation. External: growth that also involves another organisation.
b) Mergers, by agreement; takeovers, when one company obtains full control of another.
c) Horizontal: at same stage of production. Vertical: at different stage of production. Lateral: firms in different industries.
2. Economies of scale; greater chance of survival.

SUPPORTING BUSINESS

government **helps** → firms ⟶ income
protection
training
location
interest rates
trade

THE RANGE OF GOVERNMENT SUPPORT GIVEN

- <u>Financial</u> support comes mainly from central government and from the European Union.

- Examples include financial support for the less economically well off <u>regions</u> of the UK, and support through <u>training</u> <u>and</u> <u>employment</u> <u>schemes</u> such as the New Deal scheme.

- Governments consider the effect on business when changing their <u>taxation</u> and <u>interest</u> <u>rate</u> policies.

- Government <u>legislation</u> helps protect firms against unfair competition.

- Local and national government provide support through <u>information</u>.

- The government's <u>Office</u> <u>for</u> <u>National</u> <u>Statistics</u> <u>(ONS)</u> publishes a range of important statistical summaries that organisations use as information sources. These include: Regional Trends; Social Trends; and Economic Trends.

- Support for <u>exporters</u> comes from British Trade International, which gives information, advice and assistance.

- The Export Credit Guarantee Department provides guarantees and insurance against losses through exporting.

THE DTI

The <u>Department</u> <u>for</u> <u>Trade</u> <u>and</u> <u>Industry</u> (<u>DTI</u>) supports UK firms in different ways. Examples include:

- help for <u>small</u> <u>businesses</u> through its Small Business Service and Small Firms Loan Guarantee Scheme
- providing information and advice on EU developments
- offering free booklets and 'best practice' guides
- supporting firms wishing to use new computer and communications technologies.

Examiner's Top Tip
Many of the organisations that provide support for business also seek to control it.

THE EUROPEAN UNION

- **The EU offers <u>financial</u> <u>support</u> through funds such as its Regional Development Fund, which helps support poorer regions.**
- **The EU also provides support through <u>information</u>.**
- **The <u>Single</u> <u>Market</u> is probably the greatest assistance given to efficient UK firms, through removing trade barriers and allowing free access to EU markets.**

Examiner's Top Tip
Remember that other organisations, such as chambers of commerce and the Confederation of British Industry (CBI), also support UK business.

INTERNET

There are many places that offer support for businesses; these are some of them:
www.dti.gov.uk/support/index.htm
www.dti.gov.uk/europe/index.htm
www.dti.gov.uk/ca/default.htm
www.ukonlineforbusiness.gov.uk

Examiner's Top Tip
The EU is an increasingly important influence: link your study of it with this section (see also pages 10–11).

QUICK TEST

1. List three areas of assistance given to UK businesses by the UK government.
2. Give two reasons why the UK government wishes to support UK firms.
3. Name two publications issued by the ONS.

1. Financial; information; exporting.
2. To remain competitive internationally; to encourage employment.
3. Regional Trends; Social Trends.

PROTECTING CONSUMERS

Since individual consumers are usually in a weak bargaining position with the large organisations they buy from, there are many UK and EU laws to protect them.

- The <u>Sale</u> and <u>Supply</u> of <u>Goods</u> <u>Act</u> (1994) requires goods that are sold to:
  – be of <u>satisfactory quality</u>
  – be <u>fit</u> <u>for</u> <u>the</u> <u>purpose</u> for which they are intended
  – <u>match</u> <u>their</u> <u>description</u>
- The <u>Supply</u> of <u>Goods</u> <u>and</u> <u>Services</u> <u>Act</u> (1982) extends sales of goods law to services
- The <u>Trade</u> <u>Descriptions</u> <u>Acts</u> (1968, 1972) make it a criminal offence to give a false description of goods
- EU <u>Directives</u> also protect consumers. For example, there are directives on:
  – <u>Electronic</u> <u>Commerce</u> (information providers must provide certain information to users of e-commerce)
  – <u>Price</u> <u>Indication</u> (selling prices and other details must be displayed)
  – <u>Misleading</u> <u>Advertising</u> (protection against unfair adverts)
  – <u>CE</u> <u>Marking</u> (products meeting safety and other standards can carry the CE mark).

PROTECTING EMPLOYEES

Individual employees are also in a weak position compared with their employers. As a result, UK and EU laws safeguard employees, particularly in the areas of <u>employment</u>, <u>discrimination</u>, and <u>health</u> <u>and</u> <u>safety</u>.

EMPLOYMENT

Employees working under a contract of employment are protected against <u>unfair</u> <u>dismissal</u>.

The EU is a major influence on employment law. Recent examples include:

- limiting working time to a normal maximum of 48 hours per week
- giving employees the right to unpaid leave following the birth of a child
- ensuring equal treatment for part-time staff.

DISCRIMINATION

There are several important Acts protecting workers against discrimination. These include:

- the <u>Race</u> <u>Relations</u> <u>Acts</u> (1968 and 1976), which make it illegal to discriminate on the grounds of race, nationality or ethnic origin
- the <u>Disability</u> <u>Discrimination</u> <u>Act</u> (1995), which makes it unlawful to discriminate against a person on the grounds of disability
- the <u>Equal</u> <u>Pay</u> <u>Act</u> (1970) and the <u>Sex</u> <u>Discrimination</u> <u>Acts</u> (1975 and 1987), which seek to protect women against unequal pay and treatment compared with men.

HEALTH

The <u>Health</u> <u>and</u> <u>Safety</u> <u>at</u> <u>Work</u> <u>Act</u> (1974) outlines duties concerning matters of health and safety. The employer must provide safe:

- working conditions
- machinery
- working processes
- entry and exit.

In return, employees must take reasonable care of themselves and others at work, not interfere with safety items, notify the employer of safety problems, and co-operate with the employer concerning safety matters.

PROTECTING COMPETITION

<u>Monopolies</u> – where one firm dominates a market – are discouraged, because the monopoly firm can set its own prices (no competition) and exploit consumers. The UK government encourages competition through the <u>Price</u> <u>Mechanism</u>, with its interaction of supply and demand.

- The <u>Fair</u> <u>Trading</u> <u>Act</u> (1973) set up the <u>Office</u> <u>of</u> <u>Fair</u> <u>Trading</u> (OFT), which can examine the trading activities of a firm.
- The <u>Competition</u> <u>Act</u> (1980) protects firms against the anti-competitive practices of other firms.
- The <u>Competition</u> <u>Commission</u> works with the OFT to ensure that proposed mergers between large companies are in the interests of consumers.
- The EU's competition policy seeks to protect consumers against unfair monopolies.

BUSINESS AND THE LAW

KEY POINTS

All organisations face various controls through laws, rules and regulations. Other laws exist to protect people and other firms who are involved with the organisation.

Activities that are <u>controlled</u> include:
- where the organisation operates $\Rightarrow$ controlling its <u>location</u> and its <u>development</u>
- what it has to pay $\Rightarrow$ controlling its <u>tax</u>

Areas of <u>protection</u> include
- people with whom it deals $\Rightarrow$ protecting its <u>employees</u> and its <u>customers</u>
- those who share its marketplace $\Rightarrow$ protecting its <u>competitors</u>

Examiner's Top Tip
You may be asked to explain <u>why</u> protection is needed as well as what protection is available.

QUICK TEST

1. Employees are protected against exploitation by their employers in the areas of e_____, d_____ and h_____.

2. Why are monopolies discouraged in the UK economy?

3. In what ways does sales of goods law protect the purchaser of goods?

3. Goods must be of satisfactory quality, fit for their intended purpose, and – if sold by description – must match their description.
2. Lack of competition can lead to higher prices and exploitation of consumers.
1. Employment, discrimination, health and safety.

PRESSURE GROUPS

- A 'pressure group' is an organised group of people who share similar interests, and who wish to further their interests by influencing others.
- A pressure group may be a <u>local</u> organisation, such as a local residents' association campaigning against noise or pollution from a local factory.
- The group may be <u>national</u>, such as the Automobile Association, which campaigns mainly on behalf of UK motorists, or <u>international</u> (e.g. Greenpeace or Friends of the Earth).
- <u>Trade</u> <u>unions</u> have been influential pressure groups for many years, through acting on behalf of their members.
- The <u>TUC</u> (Trades Union Congress) and the <u>CBI</u> (Confederation of British Industry) are national pressure groups campaigning for unions and employers respectively, hoping to influence government and EU policy.
- In recent years, other pressure groups have had a large influence on the work of business. <u>Environmental</u> <u>pressure</u> <u>groups</u> in particular have persuaded firms to change policies and production methods.
- Many companies have responded by creating their own <u>ethical</u> <u>policies</u>. These policies often outline ways in which the company could avoid exploitation of 'third world' people and resources.

Examiner's Top Tip
When referring to green issues in your answer, concentrate on their business effects.

INTERNET

The Advertising Standards Authority website:
www.asa.org.uk

Examiner's Top Tip
Learn a definition of 'pressure group'.

CONSUMER ORGANISATIONS

- *The UK government has set up many 'watchdogs' that <u>regulate</u> our major industries, many of which were once nationalised; but which still remain potential monopolies.*
- *These regulators protect consumers and others from exploitation by organisations in industries such as water, power and telecommunications.*

Examples of organisations that support the consumer include:
- *the <u>Citizens Advice Bureau</u>, an organisation with offices in most towns where voluntary staff help consumers with a range of problems*
- *the <u>Advertising Standards Authority</u> (ASA), which is financed by the advertising industry and which oversees advertising (other than on TV or radio).*

STEP – SOCIAL, TECHNOLOGICAL, ECONOMIC AND POLITICAL – INFLUENCES

- Social influences are important because businesses now recognise the importance of a good image.
- This image is helped when the business recognises the social responsibility it has, for example to its customers, employees and shareholders.
- These influences also include changes in society (e.g. tastes and fashion).
- Changing social trends also include the increase in the average age of the population, which influences the demand for different goods and services.
- Technological developments have made some industries grow rapidly, such as the telecommunications industry with its mobile-phone market, and have forced other industries to adapt (e.g. banking, to electronic funds transfer).
- Economic influences include the level of consumer demand for a firm's goods or services.
- Government economic policy, such as its influence on interest rates (the cost of borrowing) is also important.
- The government's political policies, creating new laws that affect business, are a major influence on firms.

OTHER INFLUENCES ON BUSINESS

Social **T**echnological **E**conomic **P**olitical

QUICK TEST

1. a) One example of a social influence is: _____.
   b) One example of a technological influence is: _____.
   c) One example of an economic influence is: _____.
   d) One example of a political influence is: _____.
2. In what ways do trade unions seek to influence firms?
3. What is a pressure group?

3. An organised group of people who share similar interests, and who wish to further their interests by influencing others.
2. Through improving the pay and working conditions of their members.
1. a) changing tastes; b) new production methods; c) change in interest rates; d) new consumer protection law.

EXAM QUESTIONS — Use the questions to test your progress. Check your answers on page 94.

1. The formal structure of a large organisation is shown by its:
a) market share ☐
b) balance sheet ☐
c) mission statement ☐
d) organisation chart ☐

2. Safety standards for manufacturers are set by government and EU:
a) accounts ☐
b) taxes ☐
c) laws ☐
d) statistics ☐

3. Email has become a popular method of communicating information. Identify which of these are advantages of sending emails, and which are disadvantages:
a) transmission is instantaneous
b) large amounts of information can be sent
c) users must have a computer
d) multiple copies of the email can be sent
e) no hard copy is immediately available.

4. Classify each of the following forms of integration:
a) two insurance companies merging
b) an oil company takes over a chain of petrol stations
c) a tobacco company takes over a food processing company
d) a high-street clothing retailer takes over a clothing manufacturer
e) a newspaper group buys a competitor publisher's business.

Horizontal	Vertical forwards	Vertical backwards	Lateral

5. For each of the following situations, identify the most appropriate law:
i) Brian's job advert states 'white people only'
ii) Jenny and Mike do exactly the same job, but Mike receives a higher salary
iii) Jason blocks open a fire door
iv) Sarah is not considered for promotion because she is female
v) John asks to see his personnel records
vi) Natalie refuses to attend training on fire prevention
vii) A wheelchair user wants to talk to the directors about difficult access to work

a) Sex Discrimination.
b) Race Relations
c) Data Protection
d) Disability Discrimination
e) Health and Safety at Work
f) Equal Pay

6. Give **three** reasons why a company benefits from owning businesses at every stage of production.

....
....
....

7. Outline the advantages and disadvantages which membership of the EU's Single Market brings for British business.

....
....
....
....

8. This is the organisation chart for Tastystuff Ltd, a food manufacturer. Study the chart and answer the questions.

```
                          ┌──────────────┐
                          │  Managing    │
                          │  Director    │
                          └──────────────┘
        ┌──────────────┬──────────┴───────────┬──────────────────┐
 ┌────────────┐ ┌────────────┐ ┌──────────────────┐ ┌────────────┐
 │ Production │ │ Marketing  │ │ Human Resources  │ │ Financial  │
 │ Director   │ │ Director   │ │ Director         │ │ Director   │
 └────────────┘ └────────────┘ └──────────────────┘ └────────────┘
   ┌────┴────┐        │          ┌──────┴──────┐          │
┌──────┐ ┌──────────┐ ┌───────┐ ┌─────────┐ ┌──────────┐ ┌──────────────┐
│Works │ │Production│ │Sales  │ │Staff    │ │Recruit-  │ │Accounts      │
│Manager││Controller│ │Manager│ │Welfare  │ │ment      │ │Office        │
│      │ │          │ │       │ │Manager  │ │Manager   │ │Manager       │
└──────┘ └──────────┘ └───────┘ └─────────┘ └──────────┘ └──────────────┘
   │          │          │                       │              │
┌──────┐ ┌──────────┐ ┌────────┐           ┌──────────────┐ ┌──────────┐
│Works │ │Production│ │Marketing│          │Human Resources│ │Accounts  │
│Office│ │Office    │ │Office  │           │Office Staff   │ │Office    │
│Staff │ │Staff     │ │Staff   │           │               │ │Staff     │
└──────┘ └──────────┘ └────────┘           └──────────────┘ └──────────┘
```

a) Name **three** other departments or sections Tastystuff Ltd may have, but which are not shown on this chart.

....

....

b) Explain the work of the Human Resources function in Tastystuff Ltd.

....

c) Use this chart to explain the terms 'hierarchy', 'span of control' and 'chain of command'.

....

d) Explain **three** reasons why organisation charts are drawn up.

....

....

e) i) Identify **one** reason why the Accounts Office staff will need to communicate with the Human Resources Office staff.

....

ii) Suggest **two** methods of internal communication that might be used between the staff in this situation. Justify your choice.

....

iii) Explain why good communication is important to Tastystuff Ltd.

....

....

How did you do?

1–2	correct	..........start again
3–4	correct	..........getting there
5–6	correct	..........good work
7–8	correct	..........excellent

1. RECRUITING STAFF

A decision must be made whether the business recruits internally or externally for a post.

INTERNAL RECRUITMENT
- <u>Morale</u> <u>improves</u> because staff realise there are promotion opportunities available, although the morale of colleagues who did not get the job may fall.
- The person appointed <u>already</u> <u>knows</u> <u>work</u> <u>routines</u> and procedures.
- Recruitment <u>costs</u> <u>are</u> <u>lower</u>, but <u>no</u> <u>new</u> <u>ideas</u> from outside will be introduced into the business.

EXTERNAL RECRUITMENT
- Although <u>more</u> <u>costly</u>, there will be a <u>wider</u> <u>range</u> <u>of</u> <u>applicants</u> from which to choose.
- Recruiting externally brings in <u>new</u> <u>blood</u> and new ideas.

With internal recruitment, <u>Human</u> <u>Resource</u> <u>Management</u> (HRM) staff must bring the post to the attention of all employees. This is usually done by using notice-boards, staff magazines or circulars (e.g. by email). When advertising externally for staff, the business can choose from various sources.
- <u>Newspapers</u> <u>and</u> <u>magazines</u> – national papers and specialist magazines for professional posts, and local papers for less high-level and specialist staff.
- <u>Jobcentres</u> – these provide employment advice as well as having details of local jobs.
- <u>Employment</u> <u>agencies</u> – these businesses will try to find suitable employees – for a fee – when asked to do so by a local employer.
- <u>Direct</u> <u>contact</u> – businesses may contact schools, colleges or training agencies for staff.

2. SELECTING STAFF

HRM staff study the work records of internal applicants. They will send external applicants an **application form**, or ask these applicants to submit their **CVs** (Curriculum Vitae). After all applications are received, a **shortlist** will be drawn up by comparing applicants with the post's job description and person specification.

Applicants are normally **interviewed**.
- Although this is **expensive** for the business, the interviewer can assess the interviewee's appearance, confidence and knowledge, and ask relevant questions
- Interview is a **two-way** **process**, since the interviewee also has the chance to ask questions.

Sometimes **selection** **tests** are set at interview. These include:
- **aptitude** **tests** to see if the candidate can do the work required
- **intelligence** **tests** designed to check the candidate's mental abilities
- **personality** **tests** to discover the applicant's personality type.

Examiner's Top Tip
The difference between job description and person specification is a popular test topic.

3. APPOINTING STAFF

The HRM staff will take up and check the successful applicant's <u>references</u>, and later issue a <u>contract</u> <u>of</u> <u>employment</u>. The contract contains:
- names of employer and employee, and the start date of the employment
- details of hours, pay, pension, sick pay, holidays and holiday pay
- the length of notice required
- disciplinary rules.

KEY POINTS

Why recruit staff?

Many businesses draw up a <u>workforce plan</u> to help them meet future staffing needs, as people leave by retiring or resigning. A workforce plan is particularly valuable in helping the business cope with <u>changing employment patterns</u>, such as:

- the increase in part-time employment
- more women seeking work
- an ageing population.

Job analysis

This is used to find out the various tasks and responsibilities of a particular job. It consists of two main elements.

- The <u>job description</u> contains the job title, details of where it is based, with whom the job holder will work, and a summary of the main activities.
- The <u>person</u> (or <u>job</u>) <u>specification</u> lists the qualifications, experience and skills a person will need to carry out the job.

When advertising for new employees, the HRM staff need to make sure that the wording of any adverts must obey <u>legal requirements</u> concerning racial, sexual and disability discrimination.

Examiner's Top Tip
You may still find the term 'Personnel' used to describe the work of the HRM function.

EMPLOYING STAFF

QUICK TEST

1. Of which form of recruitment – internal or external – are the following characteristics? Tick the appropriate column.

	Internal recruitment	External recruitment
a) All existing staff need to be notified	☐	☐
b) Adverts for staff may be placed in newspapers	☐	☐
c) An employment agency may be used	☐	☐
d) Recruitment costs are relatively low	☐	☐

Examiner's Top Tip
You may be able to structure your answers using 'recruiting', 'selecting' and 'appointing' sections.

2. Delete which does not apply:

a) Details of the qualifications required to do the job are listed in the person specification/job description

b) The main activities to be undertaken by the post holder are listed in the person specification/job description

3. Which of these Acts will influence the work of HRM staff when recruiting new starters?

a) Race Relations Acts

b) Sex Discrimination Acts

c) Equal Pay Act

d) Disability Discrimination Act

3. All of them
2. a) 'job description'; b) 'person specification'
1. a) internal; b) external; c) external; d) internal

TRAINING AND DEVELOPING STAFF

WHY TRAIN STAFF?

- Staff training and development take place so that new and existing employees work as efficiently as possible to help the business meet its objectives.
- Staff also have to cope with <u>changes</u> to their work, e.g. as a result of technological developments, and training will be required.
- Training also prepares staff for <u>future</u> <u>promotion</u>: they 'grow' as the business grows.

Managers want new staff to contribute to the work of the business as quickly as possible, and will therefore organise <u>induction</u> <u>training</u> for the new employees. Existing staff will also need training and developing, through <u>on-the-job</u> and <u>off-the-job</u> forms, to improve their knowledge and skill levels.

The business also gains through creating a <u>good</u> <u>reputation</u> as well as ensuring it has <u>staff</u> <u>with</u> <u>the</u> <u>right</u> <u>skills</u>.

INDUCTION TRAINING

This training introduces the firm to the new employee, and the new employee to the firm. The new employees need to learn about:
- the firm's <u>objectives</u>, its <u>working practices</u> and its <u>rules</u>
- their <u>role</u> and <u>responsibilities</u> in the firm
- the <u>environment</u> in which they will be working.

The length of the induction depends on the <u>importance</u> and degree of <u>difficulty</u> of the job.

APPRAISAL

Most entrepreneurs recognise the value of improving employees' skills. An appraisal system is used to identify an individual employee's strengths and weaknesses. Appraisal involves:
- an <u>interview</u> between the employee and the appraiser (e.g. a <u>supervisor</u>)
- setting <u>targets</u> and identifying <u>training</u> <u>needs</u> for the employee.

ON-THE-JOB TRAINING

This _internal_ approach is the simplest form of staff training and development. The employee is trained by someone who already has the appropriate knowledge, skills and experience.
As a result:
• training and development is often _less costly_ than off-the-job training
• it will _concentrate exclusively on the needs of the business_
• but it may be of a _poor standard_ if those carrying it out are not highly skilled in training and communicating.

OFF-THE-JOB TRAINING

This **external** training usually takes place in specialist organisations, although the business may employ its own specialist training staff. Although normally **more expensive** than 'on-the-job' training, this type
• is carried out by **outside specialists**
• often leads to **new ideas** being brought into the business from outside
• is more likely to let staff being trained **work at their own pace**.

KEY POINTS

The nature, amount and quality of training carried out will depend largely on their <u>costs</u> and on the <u>resources</u> available.
• Some organisations have their own training departments, whereas others must rely on specialist training organisations or on government initiatives.
• The <u>government</u> is a major influence, e.g. in establishing

<u>Learning and Skills Councils</u>, and by creating training schemes such as the <u>Modern Apprenticeship</u> scheme.

A popular recent development is <u>trickle-down</u> or <u>cascade</u> training. A number of staff are trained externally, then return to the business and train the remaining staff.

QUICK TEST

1. Tick the correct column to show whether the following are characteristics of Internal or External training.

	Internal	External
a) Usually less costly	☐	☐
b) Specialist trainers will be employed	☐	☐
c) Devoted solely to the needs of the firm	☐	☐

Examiner's Top Tip
Point out that any programme of training must consider the needs of the business _and_ the needs of the employee.

2. In most appraisal systems, the person being appraised is i_____ to identify any t_____ n_____ and to set t_____.

3. Identify two influences on the training offered by an organisation.

3. Resources available (e.g. training staff); cost of the training.
2. interviewed, training needs, targets
1. a) internal; b) external; c) internal

THEORIES ON MOTIVATING STAFF

hygiene factors   motivators   theory X   social needs

satisfiers   self-actualisation   theory Y   security

WHY IS MOTIVATION IMPORTANT?

In business, motivation shows how satisfied or dissatisfied people are at work. If employees are motivated, they will be more likely to achieve business goals.

Nowadays, as a result of studying the work of motivational theorists, most employers accept that their staff can contribute valuable ideas, make decisions, solve problems, and take on extra responsibilities.

Examiner's Top Tip
You are often asked to explain the work of (usually two) theorists.

ABRAHAM MASLOW

This psychologist identified **five human needs** he believed people wanted to satisfy. As one set of needs was satisfied by an individual, it would stop acting as a motivator, but the individual would then be motivated by the next set of needs.

Self-actualisation
Ego
Social
Safety
Basic

Names for the need	Meaning	Relevance to business
Self-actualisation needs	The need to **fulfil your potential**	Employers allow staff to work at what they are good at, and to organise their work in the ways they wish to do it.
Ego (or **esteem**) needs	The need to be **valued**	Rewards if targets are met, merit pay rises, promotion; employers offer praise and acknowledge the good work of the employee.
Social (or acceptance) needs	The need to belong to and work in a group	Team meetings, company magazines, staff social events; employers allow their staff to work in groups.
Safety (or **security**) needs	The need to be **protected**	Safe machinery; protection in employment (e.g. a contract), and protection if the employee becomes unemployed (e.g. receiving redundancy pay).
Basic (or **physiological**) needs	Food, warmth, sleep, clothes	Heating, toilets, canteen; employees need money to buy these 'basics' such as food, so employers must pay a living wage.

Maslow's theory suggests employers should **recognise their employees have a range of different needs**, and **plan work** to meet this range of needs.

FREDERICK HERZBERG

Herzberg interviewed accountants and engineers, asking them to identify what made them feel 'good' and 'bad' about their jobs. As a result, he developed a <u>two-factor</u> theory of motivation based on hygiene factors and motivators:

- <u>Hygiene</u> <u>factors</u> include an employee's salary, and the level of job security.
- By themselves, these are not motivators, but if they are removed they act as <u>dissatisfiers</u> and will demotivate the employee (the 'bad feelings' about work).
- <u>Motivators</u> act as '<u>satisfiers</u>': these 'good feelings' include promotion, recognition and achievement at work.
- This suggests that challenging, interesting and rewarding work will motivate and satisfy employees.
- Herzberg concluded that the satisfiers relate to the job's <u>content</u> (e.g. the job itself), and dissatisfiers to the job's <u>context</u> (e.g. working conditions).
- <u>Satisfiers</u> <u>motivate</u> <u>when</u> <u>present</u>: dissatisfiers <u>demotivate</u> <u>when</u> <u>not</u> <u>present</u>.

OTHER THEORISTS

ELTON MAYO

- Mayo researched work practices, and altered the working conditions of a group of workers to study the effect on their output.
- Output rose after every change made, even when normal conditions returned at the end of the research. This showed that the main reasons for the rise in production were:
- the <u>employees</u> <u>felt</u> <u>important</u> as a result of their work being studied
- they had become <u>involved</u> in establishing their own work routines.

The work of Mayo shows that <u>group</u> <u>working</u> <u>relations</u> and employee involvement are important in motivating staff.

DOUGLAS MCGREGOR

- McGregor's '<u>Theory X</u>' manager believes that an employee dislikes work and will avoid it if possible.
- As a result, Theory X workers must be controlled, directed and threatened with punishment if necessary to make them work.
- McGregor's '<u>Theory Y</u>' manager believes that an employee finds work as natural as play or rest.
- As a result, they are able and willing to organise, control and direct themselves, and to accept authority and responsibility.
- Control and punishment are not effective ways to get the Theory Y employee to work.

McGregor's analysis shows that employers should <u>treat</u> <u>their</u> <u>employees</u> <u>as</u> <u>individuals</u>, finding out what exactly motivates them.

Examiner's Top Tip
If you discuss Maslow's work, relate his ideas to the work environment.

QUICK TEST

1. Tick the relevant column:

	Maslow	Herzberg	McGregor
Theory Y	☐	☐	☐
Hygiene factors	☐	☐	☐
Self-actualisation	☐	☐	☐
Ego needs	☐	☐	☐
Motivators	☐	☐	☐

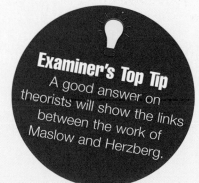

Examiner's Top Tip
A good answer on theorists will show the links between the work of Maslow and Herzberg.

2. Are these hygiene factors or motivators?

a) 'I've just received the 'Employee of the month' award'.

b) 'I've just received a five per cent increase in my hourly pay rate'.

PAYING STAFF

MONEY AND MOTIVATION

Pay is an important motivator. It enables people to buy things (e.g. to meet Maslow's basic needs), and *pay levels* are one indicator of a person's *job status* and *power*. Employers have their own pay policy, which will be influenced by:
* the accepted *rate for the job*
* the pay rates of *competitors*
* the influence of *trade unions*, e.g. through nationally agreed rates of pay.

The value of having other *non-money* forms of motivation is now recognised. These include:
* *job rotation* – allowing employees to move between jobs, especially between some of the more boring ones
* *job enrichment* – the employee's job is enriched by *restructuring* it to increase the tasks and responsibility
* *employee participation* – e.g. in quality circles and works councils, or as worker-directors.

KEY POINTS

Pay levels vary between <u>occupations</u> and between <u>regions</u>. **Reasons for these difference include:**

* the <u>cost of living</u> in the area – e.g. property and rents in south-east England tend to be expensive
* the <u>nature of work</u> – the amount of discomfort and danger influences pay levels

* the <u>qualifications and training</u> required – e.g. doctors have to train for many years
* <u>supply and demand</u> – e.g. very talented sports stars and artists receive high pay.

The government has now established a <u>minimum wage</u> in the UK. As a result, employers should not be able to exploit their staff, who should now receive at least this minimum level.

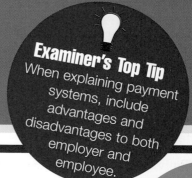

Examiner's Top Tip
When explaining payment systems, include advantages and disadvantages to both employer and employee.

WAGES AND SALARIES

Employees receive either a wage or a salary for their work. The normal differences are:

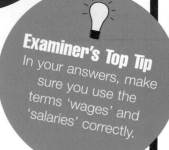

Examiner's Top Tip
In your answers, make sure you use the terms 'wages' and 'salaries' correctly.

Wages	Salaries
paid weekly	paid monthly
hourly rates often used	stated as a yearly figure
overtime often paid	overtime often not paid
associated with factories	associated with offices
usually for manual work	usually for clerical or supervisory work

CALCULATING PAY

FLAT RATE SYSTEM

- Employees receive a **fixed** **amount** for work done, such as one-twelfth of their annual salary being paid each month.
- This helps employers plan and **budget** for the amounts due, and **administration** **is** **easier**.
- There is **no** **financial** **incentive** for employees to work harder.

TIME RATE SYSTEM

- Employees receive an **agreed** **amount** **for** **each** **hour** **worked**, and may earn **overtime** at higher rates of pay.
- The **wage** **bill** **is** **more** **difficult** **to** **budget** **for** **and** **to** **calculate**, although there is a financial **incentive** **for** **staff** **to** **work** **longer** **hours**.

PIECE RATE SYSTEM

- Under this 'payment by results' approach, the employee is **paid** **for** **each** **completed** **item** **made**.
- This **encourages** **hard** **work**, but there may be **problems** **of** **quality** if employees rush their work.

COMMISSION AND BONUSES

- Employees may receive **commission** (e.g. the sales force being paid something for each item sold) as part or all of their pay.
- Employees may also be awarded **merit** **bonuses** for the quality of work done.
- These **encourage** **hard** **work** but can **demotivate**, e.g. if the bonus or commission is difficult to achieve.

SHARE OWNERSHIP AND PROFIT-SHARING SCHEMES

- Many businesses **involve** **their** **staff** through offering shares in the company at low or no cost.
- They may also offer their employees **a** **share** **of** **the** **profits**.
- These schemes increase motivation by **making** **the** **staff** **feel** **more** **involved** in the business.

Examiner's Top Tip
Remember that pay is not the only motivator for employees.

QUICK TEST

1. List three ways in which wages and salaries usually differ.
2. How does performance-related pay differ from a flat-rate system?
3. Identify one advantage of paying staff:
    a) bonuses
    b) a share of the firm's profits.

1. Period of pay (week or month); location/nature of work (e.g. factory and office); amount is variable (wage) or fixed (salary).
2. Performance-related pay is based on the number of (satisfactory) items made; flat-rate systems ignore this.
3. a) Encourages staff loyalty and hard work   b) staff feel directly involved in the success of the firm.

GROUPS IN BUSINESS

TYPES OF TRADE UNION

Unions are normally grouped under four headings.

CRAFT UNIONS
- These were the earliest unions, which supported skilled craftsmen who had learnt their trade through the unions' apprenticeship system.
- Examples include the <u>Musicians' Union</u>.

INDUSTRIAL UNIONS
- These grew out of the traditional heavy industries, such as steel, coal and railways.
- Examples include <u>USDAW</u>, a union for workers in shops and the distribution industry.

GENERAL UNIONS
- These usually have large memberships, often from semi-skilled and unskilled occupations.
- Examples include <u>UNISON</u>, a general union for public sector employees.

'WHITE-COLLAR' UNIONS
- These are the most recently formed unions, due to the growing numbers of people working in clerical and administrative occupations.
- Examples include teaching unions such as the <u>National Union of Teachers</u>.

THE TUC, THE CBI AND OTHER ORGANISATIONS

Examiner's Top Tip
The role of the unions is a popular exam topic.

The <u>Trades Union Congress</u> (TUC) represents the views of those unions that are <u>affiliated</u> (joined) to it.
- As the national body that speaks for organisations with millions of workers, the TUC seeks to <u>influence government policy</u>, e.g. on political, economic and social issues.

The <u>Confederation of British Industry</u> (CBI) is to employers what the TUC is to unions. It <u>represents employers</u> in both the private and public sectors.
- it seeks to persuade <u>government</u> to follow policies supported by the CBI
- it provides <u>advice</u> and <u>assistance</u> to its members.

<u>Employers' associations</u>, like trade unions, were first formed to protect the interests of their members. Their role includes <u>representing employers</u> in wage negotiations and other discussions. Again, like unions, they have <u>increased the range of their activities</u>, e.g. providing legal advice and assistance. Examples include:
- the National Farmers' Union
- the Road Haulage Association
- the Society of Motor Manufacturers and Traders.

UNION AIMS, STRUCTURE AND MEMBERSHIP

The main <u>aim</u> of a trade union is to <u>carry</u> <u>out</u> <u>activities</u> <u>to</u> <u>support</u> <u>the</u> <u>interests</u> <u>of its</u> <u>members</u>. It seeks to do this through:

· improving <u>pay levels</u> for the members
· improving their <u>working conditions</u>
· protecting their <u>jobs</u>
· offering <u>services</u> such as help with legal and financial matters
· being involved in <u>decision-making</u> in the workplace.

The typical union <u>structure</u> is:

· <u>national</u> – at the Head Office, the union's Executive, normally led by the General Secretary, will decide union policy and represent the union nationally, e.g. in the media and at national wage negotiations
· <u>regional</u> – the union employs representatives to work at a regional level, supporting branches and providing expertise, e.g. on legal matters
· <u>branch</u> – union members at the workplace are often represented by a shop steward, who is unpaid.

National

Regional

Local (branch)

www.cbi.org.uk/home.html
www.tuc.org.uk

KEY POINTS

Why do trade unions exist? The fact that, in the past, some business owners treated their employees unfairly led to the employees joining together to form unions that would protect their interests. The most important role today for unions is often to <u>protect</u> <u>their</u> <u>members'</u> <u>rights</u> <u>under</u> <u>the</u> <u>law</u>.

In recent years, two trends have been for:
• union <u>membership</u> <u>to</u> <u>fall</u> – reasons include a) fewer jobs in those manufacturing industries where union membership is traditionally high, and b) difficulty in recruiting union members from the expanding service sector
• unions to <u>merge</u> – this gives them greater bargaining power.

Union members gain <u>protection</u>, access to <u>expertise</u> in areas such as employment law, and a range of other <u>benefits</u>.

QUICK TEST

1. Classify these unions:

a) BALPA (a union for airline pilots)

b) NUJ (National Union of Journalists)

c) BECTU (a union for people in broadcasting, film and cinema)

d) GMB ('General, Municipal and Boilermakers')

e) MOMIMTS (Military and Orchestral Musical Instrument Makers Trade Society)

2. List four main aims of trade unions.

3. What aims do the TUC and CBI share?

3. To support their member organisations; to persuade the government to adopt the policies they support.
2. Improve pay, improve conditions, protect members, provide services for members.
1. a) White-collar (or industrial)   b) industrial   c) industrial   d) general   e) craft.

COLLECTIVE BARGAINING

Collective bargaining involves <u>negotiations</u> <u>between</u> <u>employers</u> (or their associations) <u>and</u> <u>unions</u> or other worker representatives. These negotiations usually involve the employees' <u>pay</u> and their <u>working conditions</u>. Collective bargaining may occur within a single company, or at a national level. More collective bargaining is now being carried out at a local level, because:
- more people are employed on temporary or part-time contracts
- many companies have 'single union' agreements, where only one union is recognised.

WORKING TOGETHER

INDUSTRIAL ACTION

Sometimes <u>disputes</u> occur between employers and unions representing employees. A dispute may result in <u>industrial</u> <u>action</u>, taken by union members to persuade employers to agree to the union's wishes.

- <u>Overtime</u> <u>bans</u> – members refuse to work overtime, which will <u>reduce</u> <u>output</u> and may lead to orders not being met

- <u>Work-to-rule</u> – union members are careful to follow every rule, which may also reduce work output.

- <u>Go-slow</u> – members carry out their work more slowly than normal, but still work within the terms of their contract.

There are different forms of industrial action:

- <u>Picketing</u> – union members stand outside the firm to persuade their fellow employees not to attend work.

- <u>Strikes</u> – union members withdraw their labour by refusing to go to work.

- <u>Sit-ins</u> – this is where a group of union members occupies the firm's buildings to publicise their protest and persuade managers to meet their demands.

Strikes usually receive the most publicity. They are not popular with employers – due to the effect on production – or with union members, who lose pay. Strikes are normally <u>official</u>:
- the union must <u>ballot</u> its members on this form of industrial action
- if members vote for a strike, the union then informs managers of the plan to hold a strike.

SETTLING DISPUTES

Managers and those employees in dispute will want to end – <u>resolve</u> – it. The services of <u>ACAS</u> – the Advisory, Conciliation and Arbitration Service – may be used. Set up in 1975, ACAS tries to <u>improve</u> <u>industrial</u> <u>relations</u>. It does this by offering:

- a <u>conciliation</u> service – an ACAS official will discuss the dispute with both groups, to find where there is already agreement so that more negotiation can take place
- an <u>arbitration</u> service – when the groups in dispute 'go to arbitration', they agree to accept the ruling of an independent third party (provided by ACAS) who listens to both sides and then states how the dispute will be settled
- <u>information</u> and <u>advice</u> – ACAS has a number of information centres to help people with enquiries about employment law.

Employees, with the support of their unions, may take their dispute to <u>industrial</u> <u>tribunals</u>.
- The tribunal can arrange for an employee who has been dismissed unfairly to be <u>reinstated</u> (re-employed) at work.
- It may also award <u>monetary</u> <u>compensation</u> to employees who have been treated unfairly.

KEY POINTS

As a result of industrial action, employers may find:
- <u>customers</u> are lost – loss of production leads to loss of sales, which causes the organisation's customers to look elsewhere for an alternative supplier
- <u>cash</u> <u>flow</u> becomes a problem – lower sales means lower sales revenue, and a business facing industrial action may also find it difficult to raise finance if its reputation suffers because of the action
- low <u>employee</u> <u>morale</u> – industrial action leads to poor industrial relations, which will affect the quality of employees' work and their relationship with the employer.

QUICK TEST

1. What is the purpose of collective bargaining?

2. List six different forms of industrial action.

3. The three ways ACAS seeks to improve industrial relations and solve disputes are through offering a c_____ service, an a_____ service and by giving general a_____.

Examiner's Top Tip
Learn a definition of collective bargaining.

3. Conciliation, arbitration, advice.
2. Overtime ban, work-to-rule, go-slow, picketing, sit-in, strike.
1. Employers and employees (e.g. through their union) negotiate pay and conditions.

EXAM QUESTIONS — Use the questions to test your progress. Check your answers on page 94.

1. List **three** key aspects of a company's Human Resources function.

....
....
....

2. People selected for interview are put on:
a) an account ☐
b) an agenda ☐
c) a short-list ☐
d) a payroll ☐

3. The details of a new full-time employee's work are shown in the:
a) final accounts ☐
b) contract of employment ☐
c) job description ☐
d) person specification ☐

4. Where should these be placed in Maslow's hierarchy?
a) 'Employee of the month' award..
b) staff social event..
c) rest breaks...
d) guards being replaced on machinery..

5. List the main stages in training.

....

6. Merchant Ltd has an induction scheme for new starters. It also offers both on-the-job and off-the-job training for existing staff.

a) i) Identify **one** advantage to the company as a result of recruiting staff from outside.

....

ii) What factors will influence Merchant Ltd's success at recruiting staff from outside?

....

b) i) Name **three** items likely to be included in Merchant Ltd's induction programme.

....
....

ii) State **two** advantages to the company of having induction programmes.

....
....

c) Suggest **two** reasons why Merchant Ltd's staff may prefer off-the-job training.

....
....

7. Osborne Ltd is a manufacturing company making components used in cars and vans. The directors are planning to move their warehouse from its present location to a new site about 30 km away. Staff working in the warehouse are upset about the proposed move, and have contacted their union representatives. The trade unions at Osborne Ltd have recently negotiated a 'no-strike' agreement, in return for higher-than-average pay increases for their members.
a) What is the role of trade unions concerning the possible move of the warehouse?

....

b) In addition to the roles of the union outlined above, explain **one** other likely area of trade union involvement at Osborne Ltd.

....
....

c) Identify and explain the nature of **two** other forms of industrial action the unions could advise their members to undertake.

....
....

d) Outline the role of ACAS in resolving industrial disputes.

....
....

8. This is a job advert for a shop assistant:

> # WANTED
> ## Full-time SHOP ASSISTANT
> We are looking for an outgoing young man with a pleasant personality, who gets on well with members of the public.
> We offer pleasant working conditions and a good rate of pay. Overtime is possible.
> Full training will be given to the successful applicant.

a) Suggest **one** criticism of the advert's content.

....
....

b) Identify **three** other items of information you would expect to see in the advert.

....
....
....

c) i) Identify the payment system mentioned in the advert.

....
....

.

ii) Describe an alternative payment system suitable for this position.

....
....
....
....
....

How did you do?

1–2	correct	start again
3–4	correct	getting there
5–6	correct	good work
7–8	correct	excellent

FINANCE FOR BUSINESS

WHY IS FINANCE NEEDED?

All organisations need finance:

- to <u>start</u> in business – to do this, they need <u>assets</u> which they must buy

- to <u>survive</u> – the <u>cash inflows</u> of a business must match their <u>cash outflows</u>, and if this doesn't happen over a period of time the business will not be able to pay its way

- to <u>grow</u> – a business needs extra finance to buy more assets and to meet expenses so that it can expand.

THE MAIN SOURCES OF FINANCE

The sources of finance vary according to whether the business is in the private or the public sector. <u>Private</u> <u>sector</u> businesses have a range of sources which they can use.

INTERNAL SOURCES
- The main source of day-to-day cash comes from the business's <u>sales</u>.
- Sole traders, partners and directors of limited companies may decide to <u>keep</u> <u>profits</u> in the business, using the cash from these profits to invest in business development.
- The owners can use <u>trade</u> <u>credit</u>, delaying paying their bills to save cash.
- They can reduce <u>stock</u> <u>levels</u> to free the cash 'tied up' in these stocks.
- Businesses can sell any <u>surplus</u> <u>assets</u> they no longer need.

EXTERNAL SOURCES
- The <u>savings</u> of the owner, and/or <u>borrowing</u> from family and friends, are possible sources for sole traders and partners.
- Limited companies can issue <u>shares</u>.
- Banks arrange <u>short-term</u> <u>borrowing</u> such as overdrafts.
- <u>Loans</u> are also available from banks (and other financial institutions), are longer-term finance than overdrafts, and often have fixed repayment amounts.
- The business can <u>sell</u> <u>its</u> <u>debts</u> by 'factoring' them to a specialist firm.
- <u>Government</u> <u>grants</u> may be available, e.g. when setting up business in certain regions.
- <u>Hire</u> <u>purchase</u> and <u>leasing</u> are possible sources of extra finance.

Public sector businesses obtain their finance either directly or indirectly from the public.
- Public corporations get their finance through government grants from <u>tax</u> <u>collected</u>, and by <u>borrowing</u> from the Treasury.
- Local authority undertakings are also funded through <u>government</u> <u>grants</u>, through collecting <u>taxes</u> and <u>rates</u> from local people and businesses, and by running <u>revenue-making</u> <u>businesses</u> such as local leisure centres.

Examiner's Top Tip
Make sure you know the difference between loans (debentures) and shares, and between loans and overdrafts.

SHARES AND DEBENTURES

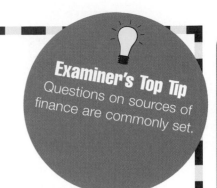

Examiner's Top Tip
Questions on sources of finance are commonly set.

These are the main sources of <u>long-term</u> <u>finance</u> available to limited companies. <u>Shares</u> are sold to people who become shareholders – <u>owners</u> – of the company.

· A <u>PLC</u> is able to advertise its shares for sale to the general public.
· A <u>private</u> <u>limited</u> <u>company</u> (ltd) must sell its shares privately.

Companies issue two main types of shares.

ORDINARY SHARES

Their owners can <u>vote</u> at the company's annual general meeting.
The dividend received by the shareholders <u>varies</u> according to the amount of profits left.
The owners receive their dividend after <u>all</u> <u>other</u> <u>debts</u> and people have been paid.
The owners are <u>last</u> to have their capital repaid if the company stops trading.

PREFERENCE SHARES

Their owners do not have a vote.
The dividend rate is <u>fixed</u> when the shares are issued.
Preference shareholders receive their dividend before ordinary shareholders.
These shareholders receive their investment back before ordinary shareholders.

Preference shares are therefore regarded as a <u>safer</u> investment than ordinary shares, although their returns may be lower if the company is successful.

<u>Debentures</u> are <u>loans</u> made to companies. They differ from shares in that:
· the debenture holders are <u>lenders</u> to, not owners of, the company
· these lenders receive a fixed <u>rate</u> <u>of</u> <u>interest</u> rather than dividends
· if the interest is not paid, the debenture holders may take <u>legal</u> <u>action</u> to recover their debts.

CHOOSING THE FINANCE

How do businesses choose from the different sources of finance available to them?
· The <u>type</u> <u>of</u> <u>project</u> for which the finance is needed is an important influence, e.g. whether it is a long-term or short-term project.
· The <u>nature</u> <u>of</u> <u>the</u> <u>business</u> is a key influence – some businesses have <u>little</u> <u>choice</u> (e.g. those in the public sector), and small firms and those businesses in high-risk areas may find their sources are limited.

QUICK TEST

1. List three reasons why businesses need finance.
2. State two differences between being a shareholder and being a debenture holder.
3. Name one:
    a) short-term source of finance
    b) medium-term source of finance
    c) long-term source of finance.

3. a) trade credit;   b) bank loan;   c) share capital
2. Shareholder – owns the company, receives dividend payments: debenture holder – lender to the company, receives interest payments.
1. To start; to survive; to expand

THE ROLE OF FINANCIAL ACCOUNTING

The <u>accountant</u> is the specialist who deals with financial accounts. The role of the accounting function is to:
- <u>collect</u> financial information from <u>original</u> <u>documents</u> such as invoices and bank statements
- <u>record</u> financial transactions in the accounts
- <u>analyse</u> this financial information, e.g. by using <u>accounting</u> <u>ratios</u>
- <u>communicate</u> this information to fellow managers
- <u>make</u> <u>decisions</u> on financial matters.

The financial accounts are normally divided into:
- the <u>sales</u> <u>ledger</u> – records of customers who buy the business's products on credit
- the <u>purchases</u> <u>ledger</u> – records of those who supply the business on credit
- the <u>cash book</u> – cash and bank records
- the <u>main</u> (also known as the <u>general</u> or <u>nominal</u>) ledger – all the other accounts of the business.

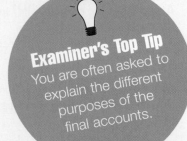

Examiner's Top Tip
You are often asked to explain the different purposes of the final accounts.

THE FINANCIAL STATEMENTS

This term is used nowadays to describe the organisation's <u>final</u> <u>accounts</u>. Private sector businesses prepare these financial statements.

THE TRADING, PROFIT AND LOSS ACCOUNT
- *This shows the business's <u>financial</u> <u>performance</u>.*
- *Profit is the difference between its <u>revenue</u> (e.g. from sales) and its <u>expenses</u>, such as the cost of any raw materials, wages and salaries, and selling and distribution costs.*
- *The <u>trading</u> account calculates the business's <u>gross</u> <u>profit</u>, the difference between its turnover and what these sales have cost the business.*
- *The <u>profit</u> <u>and</u> <u>loss</u> account is used to deduct all other expenses from the gross profit, leaving the <u>net</u> <u>profit</u> for the business.*

	£
sales	40 000
less cost of sales	15 000
gross profit	25 000
less expenses	5000
net profit	20 000

THE BALANCE SHEET
- *This shows the business's <u>financial</u> <u>position</u> by listing its <u>assets</u> (what it <u>owns</u>) and <u>liabilities</u> (what it <u>owes</u>).*

	£	£
fixed assets		200 000
current assets	75 000	
current liabilities	25 000	
		50 000
		250 000
capital and reserves		250 000

Many businesses also have to produce a <u>cash</u> <u>flow</u> <u>statement</u>. The purpose of this statement is to <u>summarise</u> <u>the</u> <u>cash</u> <u>inflows</u> <u>and</u> <u>outflows</u> that have taken place during the trading period. It includes cash movements from:
- *trading activities*
- *buying and selling assets*
- *receiving or repaying long-term capital*
- *paying share dividends.*

PUBLISHED ACCOUNTS

The directors of a public limited company must publish its financial statements (final accounts). This means that these accounts are available to members of the public, and also to the PLC's competitors. The PLC will therefore normally only show in its published accounts the minimum information required by law.

A PLC will also publish supporting statements with its accounts. These include:
- the chairman's statement, outlining the company's successes in the year
- the directors' report on the company's performance
- an auditors' report stating that the accounts have been checked by them
- a five-year summary of the company's financial performance.

Examiner's Top Tip
Net profit is a more important figure than gross profit: it is the final profit.

QUICK TEST

Match each item in column A with the correct item in column B.

A	B
a) gross profit	i) suppliers' records
b) cash flow statement	ii) list of assets and liabilities
c) sales ledger	iii) written review of the company performance
d) cash book	iv) summary of cash inflows and outflows for the year
e) balance sheet	v) net profit
f) profit & loss account	vi) bank and cash accounts
g) purchases ledger	vii) sales less the cost of those sales
h) directors' report	viii) customers' records

a) vii; b) iv; c) viii; d) vi; e) ii; f) v; g) i; h) iii.

INTERPRETING BUSINESS ACCOUNTS

Stakeholders Turnover Return on Capital Working Capital

Liquidity   Acid test   Ratios   Profit margins   Creditors

THE USERS OF FINANCIAL INFORMATION

Many stakeholder groups are interested in a business's financial performance. The groups are:

- actual and potential shareholders and other investors, who want to assess profitability of investing in the business
- lenders such as creditors and banks, who want to make sure they will get their money back, and will therefore check the business's liquidity
- managers, who will want to assess the overall performance of the business
- employees, who are interested in how safe their jobs are
- the government, which will want to be paid VAT and other taxes
- the local community, interested in the financial success or failure of the business.

PROFITABILITY RATIOS

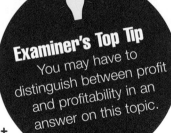

Examiner's Top Tip
You may have to distinguish between profit and profitability in an answer on this topic.

This is one key area that is examined closely when the financial performance and position of a business is being studied.

- The profitability of the business measures its profit against some other figure.
- The most important measure of profitability for a business is ROCE – its Return On Capital Employed.
- This is calculated by measuring the profit as a percentage of capital employed in the business.
- This calculation tells the investors whether their investment is worthwhile.

Other profitability measures include:

- net profit margin – this measures net profit as a percentage of turnover (net sales)
- gross profit margin – this ratio calculates gross profit as a percentage of turnover.

Ratios on their own are of limited use. The main value of using ratios is when:

- trends can be seen, by comparing the business's previous performance with past figures.
- competitors' ratios are compared with those of the business.

LIQUIDITY RATIOS

The liquidity of a business shows its <u>ability</u> <u>to</u> <u>pay</u> <u>its</u> <u>debts</u> as they become due. The business's <u>current</u> <u>assets</u> – its stocks, debtors and bank and cash balances – are compared with its <u>current</u> <u>liabilities</u> (its short-term debts). Calculating the difference between current assets and current liabilities shows the business's <u>working</u> <u>capital</u>, which is an important figure when checking its liquidity.

- *The <u>current</u> ratio matches the total current assets with the total current liabilities.*
- *This shows whether or not the business can easily pay its short-term debts.*
- *The <u>acid</u> test (also known as the Quick Assets ratio) takes the stock figure off the current assets, and then compares the result against the total current liabilities.*
- *This is often regarded as a better indicator of the liquidity position.*

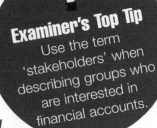

Examiner's Top Tip
Use the term 'stakeholders' when describing groups who are interested in financial accounts.

EFFICIENCY RATIOS

Examiner's Top Tip
Memorise the users of financial information, and the reasons why each group will be interested.

1. Rate of stock turnover = $\dfrac{\textbf{cost of sales}}{\textbf{average stock}}$

This shows how many times stock is 'turned over' (sold) in the period.

2. Debtors' collection period = $\dfrac{\textbf{debtors x 365}}{\textbf{sales}}$

This calculation shows how long debtors (customers buying on credit) are taking to pay the business.

3. Creditors' collection period = $\dfrac{\textbf{creditors x 365}}{\textbf{purchases}}$

This calculation shows the length of time (in days) the business takes to pay its creditors (suppliers on credit).

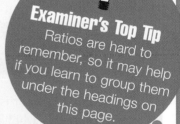

Examiner's Top Tip
Ratios are hard to remember, so it may help if you learn to group them under the headings on this page.

QUICK TEST

1. Tick the appropriate column:

	Internal stakeholders	External stakeholders
a) Managers	☐	☐
b) Shareholders	☐	☐
c) Employees	☐	☐
d) Banks	☐	☐

2. What is the difference between 'profit' and 'profitability'?

3. Name two ratios used to measure a company's liquidity.

3. Current ratio; Quick Assets ratio

2. Profit states how much the business has earned; profitability measures this profit against the resources (capital employed) used in making it.

a) internal; b) external; c) internal; d) external

maintenance   finance costs

                              advertising

    wages and salaries

    raw materials
                              administration

    delivery costs

            light, heat and power

COST BEHAVIOUR

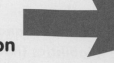

Some costs change as a business's output changes, but other costs may not be affected by these changes.

- A <u>variable</u> cost is one that changes in direct proportion to output.
- Popular examples are the cost of raw materials and piece-rate labour used to make the product.
- A <u>fixed</u> cost stays the same even though output may change.
- Examples include the rent and rates, and office salaries, paid by the business.
- In practice, many costs are <u>semi-variable</u> (or <u>semi-fixed</u>): they are affected by changes in output, but will only partly change as the output changes.
- Examples often include power costs, which have a fixed <u>standing charge</u> as well as a '<u>pay per unit</u>' charge (the variable cost).
- This analysis is important in helping accountants make decisions, and in <u>break-even analysis</u>.

STANDARD COSTING

Many organisations establish what the cost of their products <u>should be</u>. In doing so, they set <u>standards</u> for the costs of the different items making up the product.

- The <u>actual</u> costs of making the product are then paid out and recorded.
- The actual cost of materials, labour and overheads is then <u>compared with the standard</u> ('expected') cost: these differences are called <u>variances</u>.
- The variances can be studied to see why the difference has occurred.
- Variances often occur in the price or quantity of materials used, and in the cost or efficiency of the labour force.

OPPORTUNITY COST

An opportunity cost is a way of studying something a business might have done instead of what it has chosen to do. The opportunity cost is <u>not being able to do this something else</u> (because the business resources are limited).

- For example, the owners of a business might have the choice of either investing surplus cash in a new machine, or in developing a new product.
- If they decide to invest in the machine, the opportunity cost of doing so is not developing the new product.
- Opportunity cost therefore helps managers make <u>rational decisions</u> by examining the various options they have.

COSTS IN BUSINESS

DIRECT AND INDIRECT COSTS

DIRECT COSTS
- A direct cost can be linked <u>directly</u> <u>to</u> <u>a</u> <u>product</u>: for example, the main raw material used in making the product. These are some of the <u>direct</u> costs of a car:

driver and passenger seat   **gear stick**   **driver's wheel**   **windscreen**   **tyres**

INDIRECT COSTS
- An indirect cost is one that <u>cannot</u> <u>be</u> <u>traced</u> <u>directly</u> to a particular product: e.g. canteen and office costs. Indirect costs are usually called <u>overheads</u>.
- This distinction is important when accountants try to calculate the <u>full</u> <u>cost</u> of making individual products.
- It is easy to calculate the product's direct costs, but indirect costs have to be <u>apportioned</u> – shared out – between the different products.

QUICK TEST

1. State whether these costs are likely to be i) direct or indirect, and ii) fixed or variable:

   a) Steel used to make a car body

   b) Office rent

   c) The pay of a person assembling parts on one particular product line

   d) An accountant's salary

2. Indirect costs are also known as o_____, which have to be a_____ between the different products made by the business.

3. What is the purpose of standard costing?

3. To compare actual costs with what was expected, and to study any differences (variances).
2. overheads, apportioned.
1. a) direct, variable; b) indirect, fixed; c) direct, (probably fixed) d) indirect, fixed.

BREAK-EVEN

The break-even point for a business is <u>where</u> <u>total</u> <u>revenue</u> <u>is</u> <u>the</u> <u>same</u> <u>as</u> <u>total</u> <u>costs</u>. At this point the business is making neither a profit nor a loss.

Break-even analysis analyses costs into <u>fixed</u> or <u>variable</u> types, and is valuable because it calculates the point at which the business starts making a profit.

- The break-even chart is a <u>clear</u> <u>and</u> <u>simple</u> <u>planning</u> <u>tool</u> that can help managers make decisions, e.g. if costs or revenue figures change.
- However, <u>variable</u> <u>costs</u> <u>do</u> <u>not</u> <u>always</u> <u>change</u> <u>in</u> <u>proportion</u> <u>to</u> <u>output</u> (e.g.bulk-buying discounts, or overtime paid to manufacturing employees).
- The business may also set <u>different</u> <u>selling</u> <u>prices</u> in different markets.
- Break-even analysis is difficult to use if the <u>business</u> <u>makes</u> <u>more</u> <u>than</u> <u>one</u> <u>product</u>.

CONSTRUCTING THE CHART

A company has £100 000 fixed costs. The selling price of its product is £30, and the variable cost is £10. The product's production and sales are expected to reach 10 000.

THE FIXED COST LINE
- This is plotted against the '£100 000' point on the vertical '£' axis.
- It stays parallel with the horizontal 'output' axis, because fixed costs do not change.

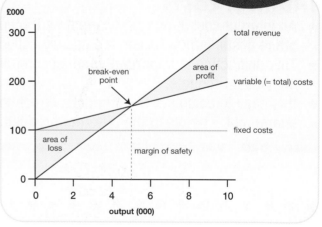

THE VARIABLE COST LINE
- This line climbs at a rate of £10 per unit of output.
- It is often plotted from the point at which the fixed cost line meets the vertical axis.
- In such cases, the variable cost line also acts as the <u>total</u> <u>cost</u> <u>line</u>.

THE SALES LINE
- This climbs from where the axes meet, at a rate of £30 for each unit of output
- The line represents the <u>total</u> <u>revenue</u> <u>line</u>.
- When this line meets the variable (total) cost line, this shows the <u>break-even</u> <u>point</u>.
- The <u>margin</u> <u>of</u> <u>safety</u> can now be calculated: this is the gap between the expected output and the break-even output, and shows <u>how</u> <u>many</u> <u>units</u> <u>sales</u> <u>can</u> <u>fall</u> <u>by</u> <u>before</u> <u>the</u> <u>business</u> <u>starts</u> <u>making</u> <u>a</u> <u>loss</u>.
- The triangle formed to the left of the break-even point represents the <u>area</u> <u>of</u> <u>loss</u>, and the triangle to the right of it the <u>area</u> <u>of</u> <u>profit</u>.
- The profit or loss at any output can now be read from the chart, both as output and as revenue.

CALCULATING THE BREAK-EVEN POINT

The normal method used to calculate the break-even point is:

total fixed costs
unit contribution

We can re-use the figures from the break-even chart on this page.
- Selling price £30 less variable cost £10 = contribution £20

- £100 000 = 5000 units (this break-even point can be seen on the chart)
  £20
- Proof: at 5000 units
  total revenue = 5000 x £30 = £150 000
  variable costs = £50 000 (5000 x £10) + fixed costs £100 000
  total costs = £150 000

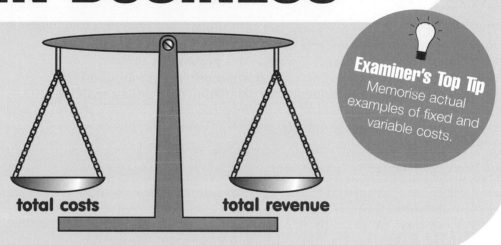

BREAKING EVEN IN BUSINESS

total costs   total revenue

Examiner's Top Tip
Memorise actual examples of fixed and variable costs.

QUICK TEST

1. An organisation's break-even point is where its t_____ c_____ are the same as its
   t_____ r_____.

2. A company selling a single product has these costs: fixed costs £350 00, variable costs £8
   per unit and selling price £15 per unit. It expects to make and sell 8 000 units. Calculate:

a) the break-even point in units and in revenue

b) the margin of safety.

1. Total costs, total revenue.
2. a) Break-even = £35 000/(£15 − £8) = 5000 units; revenue = 5000 x £15 = £75 000.
   b) Margin of safety = (8 000 − 5 000) 3 000 units.

BUDGETING IN BUSINESS

WHY BUDGET?

A budget is <u>a</u> <u>financial</u> <u>plan</u>. Managers budget for various reasons:
* *their budget makes them <u>plan</u> <u>for</u> <u>the</u> <u>future</u> resources they will need*
* *it helps them <u>check</u> <u>their</u> <u>progress</u> through comparing their actual results with those they had budgeted for*
* *this means that budgets can help <u>control</u> expenditure (this is known as <u>budgetary</u> <u>control</u>)*
* *the budget gives the manager the <u>authority</u> <u>to</u> <u>spend</u> what is in the budget.*

One of the benefits of budgeting is that it makes <u>managers</u> <u>work</u> <u>together</u> when designing their budgets, because their budgets are often linked. For example:
* *the <u>sales</u> <u>budget</u> influences figures in the <u>production</u> budget*
* *the production budget affects the <u>raw</u> <u>materials</u> <u>purchases</u> budget*
* *this purchases budget is one of the main influences on the <u>cash</u> budget.*

Budgeting is a <u>motivating</u> <u>activity</u>, especially when a manager meets the 'targets' or objectives set by the budget.

PREPARING BUDGETS

The <u>budget</u> <u>committee</u> controls the preparation of the business budgets. The procedures for preparing the budgets are usually written down in a <u>budget</u> <u>manual</u>.

The two main groups of budgets are:

* <u>operating</u> <u>budgets</u> – cash, stocks, sales, purchasing and the other budgets that come from the main operations of the business.

* <u>summary</u> <u>budgets</u> – these are budgeted final accounts:
* budgeted profit and loss
* budgeted balance sheet
* budgeted cash flow statement.

Examiner's Top Tip
Learn the definition of 'budget'. Be aware of budgeting's role in motivating staff.

CASH BUDGETING

	Jan	Feb	Mar
INFLOWS			
Sales	12 000	12 000	13 000
Bank Loan	–	5 000	–
TOTAL	12 000	17 000	13 000
OUTFLOWS			
Materials	4 000	4 500	4 500
Labour	3 000	3 200	3 200

Examiner's Top Tip
You need to be able to explain why budgeting is important in business.

The main <u>sources</u> of cash for a business are:

- capital from the owner(s)
- loans from banks and other lenders
- cash from sales
- trade credit from suppliers
- profits retained in the business.

The main <u>uses</u> of cash are:

- buying assets
- paying expenses
- paying back loan interest
- paying taxes
- allowing credit to customers.

One problem with the cash budget is that <u>it</u> <u>is</u> <u>only</u> <u>an</u> <u>estimate</u>. The managers will therefore need to check carefully the actual cash-flow that is taking place to ensure the business has enough cash to meet its bills.

QUICK TEST

1. Identify three benefits that come from budgeting.

2. Tick the relevant column:

	Source of cash	Use of cash
a) paying an electricity bill	☐	☐
b) taking out a bank loan	☐	☐
c) receiving credit from a supplier	☐	☐
d) receiving cash from goods sold	☐	☐
e) buying a delivery van	☐	☐

1. Controls expenditure; motivates managers; forces people to plan ahead.
2. Source of cash b), c) and d); Use of cash a) and e).

EXAM QUESTIONS — Use the questions to test your progress. Check your answers on pages 94–95.

1. Which of these will a company's accounts department be responsible for?

Planning production runs	Stock control
Storing finished goods	Planning an advertising campaign
Calculating financial ratios	Attracting good publicity
Appointing staff	Preparing financial statements

2. The variable costs of a business change according to which of the following:
a) taxation ☐
b) cash flow ☐
c) break even ☐
d) output? ☐

3. Which of these will be used in producing a break-even chart?
a) a balance sheet ☐
b) a cash flow forecast ☐
c) production figures ☐
d) an organisation chart ☐

4. Businesses that supply on credit are known as:
a) debtors ☐
b) creditors ☐
c) dividends ☐
d) mortgages? ☐

5. Which of these are financial statements?

a profit and loss account	an inspection schedule
a contract of employment	a cash flow statement
a job description	a stock control chart
a production planning schedule	a person specification

6. Identify and explain the importance of **two** factors that help the owners of a business decide on their sources of finance.

....

....

7. A company's production manager has forecast that 200 units of its product will be made in a week. Production costs are expected to be £51 000. The accountant has calculated that these costs will rise to £52 000 if the company makes 220 units.
a) Calculate the average cost of production of the 200 units.

....

b) Calculate the variable cost of the 20 extra units.

....

c) Explain why these two figures are different.

....

8. Suki and Scott run a partnership business. They need additional finance to pay for their materials and to obtain a new delivery van for their finished goods. Suki has agreed a bank overdraft to pay for the materials, and Scott has negotiated a loan with the garage to buy the delivery van.
Explain why each source of finance is appropriate.

....

....

....

9. A company's final accounts include these figures.

Trading, profit and loss account in £000		Balance sheet in £000	
Sales	600	Capital employed	1500
Cost of sales	450	Stock	50
Gross profit	150	Other current assets	100
Net profit	30	Current liabilities	100

a) Calculate suitable profitability and liquidity ratios.

....
....

b) Comment on your results.

....
....

c) State any other information you need to interpret your results more fully.

....
....

10. Hash Patel runs his own business, printing and selling T-shirts. He pays £3000 rent a year, and pays a part-time assistant a yearly salary of £5000. Hash has calculated that each T-shirt costs 80p to buy and 20p for the printing process. He plans to sell his T-shirts to local shops for £3 each. Hash hopes to print and sell 6000 T-shirts a year.

a) Calculate how many T-shirts Hash must buy and sell in a year to break even.

....
....

b) Construct Hash's break-even chart on a separate piece of paper.
From the chart, identify:
i) the break-even point

....

ii) Hash's break-even revenue

....

iii) the profit or loss Hash expects to make in the year

....

iv) any margin of safety for Hash.

....

How did you do?

1–2	correct .... .start again
3–4	correct .... .getting there
5–7	correct .... .good work
8–10	correct .... .excellent

METHODS OF PRODUCTION

Job production is when a business makes a single, one-off product.
- Examples include items constructed such as motorways, ships, house extensions, the Millennium Dome.
- The job is often built by skilled labour working to the customer's requirements.
- Since only one item is made, the business may not gain economies of scale.

Batch production is when more than one item at a time is made, with each batch of products being finished before the next batch (of different products) is started.
- Examples include shoes and clothing.
- Batch production is often used to make items which have a range of styles or sizes.
- The number made per batch can be based on the demand for the finished items.

Mass production (also known as flow or continuous) is when identical items are made on a production line. The product moves from one stage of production straight to the next.
- Examples include cars and consumer durables, canned foodstuffs and drinks.
- Staff and machines specialise in producing items sold on the mass market.
- Production is often highly automated, with machines replacing manual labour.

DEVELOPMENTS IN PRODUCTION

The following recent developments are now widely used by UK businesses.

JUST-IN-TIME STOCKHOLDING
This approach seeks to cut stockholding costs.
- *This can be achieved if the business operates with no buffer (reserve) stocks.*
- *It therefore runs down its stocks of raw materials, work-in-progress and finished goods.*
- *The business needs efficient ordering systems, and must have reliable suppliers.*

CELL PRODUCTION
Businesses use cell production to overcome problems of low worker morale.
- *The production line is divided into separate units (cells), each making an identifiable part of the finished product.*
- *Employees are more motivated, which increases output.*

KAIZEN
This is a Japanese term meaning 'continuous improvement'. It is based on improvement through investing in people and their ideas rather than in new technology or equipment.
- *Groups are set up to improve their own efficiency.*
- *The groups achieve this by discussing production issues, then suggesting and implementing solutions.*

LEAN PRODUCTION

Examiner's Top Tip
Lean production is a very popular exam topic.

Mass production has been criticised because
* employees can become <u>easily</u> <u>bored</u>
* machines and labour are <u>over-specialised</u>.

Lean production methods can overcome these drawbacks. This term refers to the various ways that are now used to improve the efficiency of production.

Lean production tries to <u>cut development time</u> so that the product is developed and 'on the shelves' as quickly as possible. It is often associated with <u>just-in-time</u> stock control, <u>cell production</u> and the <u>Kaizen</u> system.

PRODUCTION IN BUSINESS

Entrepreneurs need to choose the most efficient way to maketheir products. Their choice is influenced by the type of <u>product</u> they are making, and the <u>output</u> they require.

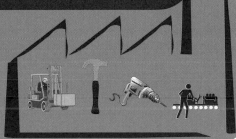

QUICK TEST

1. Tick the correct column:

	Job	Batch	Mass
a) Cans of paint	☐	☐	☐
b) A factory extension	☐	☐	☐
c) Shoes, size 7	☐	☐	☐
d) Televisions	☐	☐	☐
e) The Channel Tunnel	☐	☐	☐

2. State one advantage and one disadvantage of mass production.

1. a) mass; b) job; c) batch; d) mass; e) job;
2. Advantage: efficient use of labour and equipment. Disadvantage: employees become bored.

LARGE-SCALE BUSINESS

The costs of a business are either <u>fixed</u> or <u>variable</u>. As output goes up, the fixed costs stay the same. Although total costs will still be increasing, the average cost per unit will gradually fall. The reason is that the <u>fixed costs are spread over a larger output</u>.

- <u>Economies of scale</u> occur when the average costs of the business fall.
- This means the <u>cost per unit will be lower</u>.
- Lower unit costs make the business <u>more price competitive</u>.

ECONOMIES OF SCALE
big is ~~beautiful~~ profitable

INTERNAL ECONOMIES OF SCALE

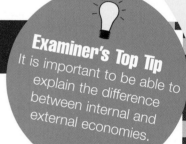
These economies are gained by a business through <u>its own growth</u>.
The main internal economies of scale are:

- <u>purchasing</u> economies – a large business can buy in bulk, paying cheaper prices for its materials and other purchases, and having greater influence over its suppliers
- <u>marketing</u> economies – although marketing and advertising costs increase, these costs are spread over much greater output
- <u>financial</u> economies – large businesses often receive loans at lower interest rates, and also find it easier to obtain these loans
- <u>technical</u> economies – a large business can afford to buy advanced and more efficient machinery and equipment, which may also replace its labour and help the business save these costs
- <u>managerial</u> economies – the larger business can employ efficient specialist managers, which will improve its decision-making
- <u>risk-bearing</u> economies – larger firms are more likely to <u>diversify</u> into different markets, and therefore are not so badly affected if sales slump in one market.

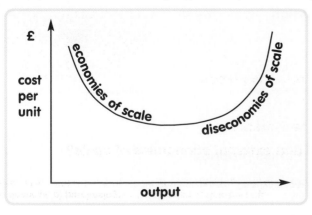

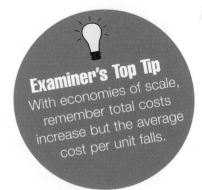

EXTERNAL ECONOMIES OF SCALE

These economies are gained by <u>all</u> businesses <u>in</u> an <u>industry</u>. The main ones are:

- economies of <u>concentration</u> – where an industry is located in one area, that area develops a <u>skilled</u> <u>labour</u> force, <u>specialist</u> <u>training</u> and <u>support</u> services for the industry
- economies of <u>information</u> – businesses in the same area may work together to obtain and share market information, and also the costs of research and development
- economies of <u>reputation</u> – the good reputation of an area will help the businesses located in that area sell their products.

DISECONOMIES OF SCALE

At some point, the business will discover that its <u>unit</u> <u>costs</u> <u>start</u> <u>to</u> <u>increase</u> again. These are diseconomies of scale. These diseconomies occur because the business cannot continue for ever becoming more cost-effective and more efficient. Reasons for diseconomies of scale include having poor:

- <u>communication</u> – as a business grows, the number of levels in their hierarchy (the 'distance' between top and bottom) increases, which slows communication down and also makes it less efficient
- <u>morale</u> <u>and</u> <u>motivation</u> – the greater 'distance' between top and bottom in the hierarchy can leave employees with a 'them and us' feeling, which can affect their work effort
- <u>co-ordination</u> – managers in larger businesses often find it more difficult to keep all functions working together effectively.

Managers can take action to prevent the effects of diseconomies of scale. For example:

Problem	Possible action
communication	improve communication systems control the amount of communication train staff in good communication practices delayer (reduce the number of levels in the hierarchy)
morale and motivation	use job rotation and job enrichment delegate more responsibility to staff
co-ordination	improve communication delayer increase spans of control

Examiner's Top Tip
Be prepared to provide examples of economies of scale.

QUICK TEST

1. Name the relevant economy of scale:

   a) a cheaper rate of interest on a bank loan

   b) a discount off raw materials when a large order is placed

   c) a specialist accountant is employed

   d) a business starts selling its products in a new market.

2. What is the main difference between internal and external economies of scale?

WHAT IS PRODUCTIVITY?

Production is the output of a business. Productivity takes this <u>output</u>, and measures it against the <u>inputs</u> used to create it. These inputs are the four factors of production – <u>land</u>, <u>labour</u>, <u>capital</u> and <u>enterprise</u> – although productivity is often measured against staff, being stated as productivity or output 'per employee'.
* Output per employee measures what a person produces in a set period of time.
* This is easy to calculate for manufacturing businesses, but less easy for businesses that provide a service.

Productivity is important because it affects the <u>costs</u> of the business, and therefore its <u>competitiveness</u>. The more productive the business gets, the more competitive it becomes because its <u>unit</u> <u>cost</u> <u>of</u> <u>production</u> <u>falls</u>.

There are two main ways to improve the productivity of a business:
* the same inputs are used more efficiently to produce a higher output
* the same output is made, but with fewer inputs.
The practical ways this is done are to:
* buy more <u>modern</u> <u>equipment</u>
* <u>train</u> <u>staff</u> to be more efficient
* <u>improve</u> <u>employee</u> <u>motivation</u>, e.g. through higher pay or greater involvement.

A popular way of increasing productivity in recent years has been to <u>substitute</u> <u>capital</u> <u>for</u> <u>labour</u>.
* This occurs when a business invests in labour-saving machinery.
* The machinery is often more productive than the employees it replaces.
* The business can now cut its labour force, and save costs by doing so.

PRODUCTIVE CAPACITY

If a business's resources are working at maximum output, it is producing at <u>full</u> <u>capacity</u>. Although full or near-full capacity means the business is operating efficiently, working at this level can cause problems for:

* <u>staff</u> – e.g. high stress levels

* <u>machines</u> <u>and</u> <u>equipment</u> – greater use can mean more frequent breakdowns.

If a business has <u>surplus</u> <u>capacity</u>, it may try to get rid of this. Ways of reducing surplus capacity include:
* not replacing staff when they leave (natural wastage)
* moving to smaller premises
* selling assets that the business no longer needs.

USING TECHNOLOGY

Capital intensity measures how much a business depends on machinery and equipment, compared with depending on labour.

- Capital intensive businesses often make products sold in <u>mass</u> <u>production</u> markets.
- Businesses in these markets can afford to buy and use expensive capital equipment.

Many businesses use advanced equipment to improve productivity.

- <u>Computer-aided</u> <u>design</u> (CAD) packages are used to create cost-effective designs for new products, or to re-style existing products.
- <u>Computer-aided</u> <u>manufacture</u> (CAM) uses robots and other hi-tech equipment to produce output efficiently and reliably.
- The use of CAD and CAM helps businesses create and make new products more and more quickly and cheaply.

Although investing in new technology may make a business more productive:

- it is <u>expensive</u> to invest in new technology
- employees may <u>resent</u> <u>changes</u> in their work practices when the new technology is introduced.

QUICK TEST

1. Productivity measures the o_____ of a business against the i_____ used to produce it. It is often stated as 'productivity p____ e_____'. Increasing productivity makes a business more c_____, because its u_____ c_____ of production f_____.

2. What is the difference between CAD and CAM?

2. CAD is concerned with the design, and CAM with the manufacture, of products.

1. Output, inputs, per employee, competitive, unit costs, fall.

QUALITY

Many businesses rely on having a quality name. They may use various quality systems.

Examiner's Top Tip
'Just-in-time' is a key idea if you are asked to explain stock and stock control.

QUALITY ASSURANCE

· makes sure that quality standards are set
· sets these standards throughout the business.

QUALITY CONTROL

· checks that the quality standards are being maintained
· tries to stop problems occurring in the first place
· identifies defects in products before these are sent to the customer.

TOTAL QUALITY MANAGEMENT (TQM)

· seeks to 'get it <u>right</u> <u>first</u> <u>time</u>' and to 'get it <u>more</u> <u>right</u> <u>next</u> <u>time</u>'
· is concerned with giving full customer satisfaction
· believes that high quality standards will reduce costs (e.g. costs of inspection)
· is closely linked with <u>Kaizen</u> ('continuous improvement') and the use of <u>quality</u> <u>circles</u>.

INTERNET

www.benchmark-research.co.uk/homepage.htm

STOCK CONTROL

All businesses hold different types of stock:

- <u>administration</u> stock – e.g. stationery and other 'consumables' used by the office staff
- <u>production</u> stock – e.g. spare parts for machines
- <u>products</u> – finished goods items ready for sales and delivery, and (for a manufacturer) raw materials in stores plus any work in progress in the factory.

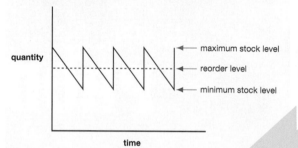

quantity — maximum stock level · reorder level · minimum stock level
time

The business has costs of <u>holding</u> stock. This encourages staff to keep stock levels as low as possible. The risk of doing this is being <u>out</u> <u>of</u> <u>stock</u>. Costs of being out of stock include:

- <u>idle</u> <u>time</u> for the employees, which must be paid for
- <u>lost</u> <u>production</u> in the factory
- <u>lost</u> <u>customers</u> and <u>poor</u> <u>reputation</u> through failing to meet orders.

To avoid these costs, managers may keep <u>stock</u> <u>levels</u> <u>high</u>. High stock levels have these costs:

- <u>working</u> <u>capital</u> (in effect, money) is 'tied up' in the stock, and is not available for use elsewhere in the business
- <u>storage</u> costs are higher
- the stock may become <u>out-of-date</u>, and may <u>deteriorate</u>
- there may be a greater risk of <u>theft</u>.

Examiner's Top Tip
Remember that quality also includes aspects such as staff training.

JUST-IN-TIME

The Just-in-time (JIT) system is associated with <u>lean</u> <u>production</u> methods.
It seeks to <u>minimise</u> <u>stock</u> by:
- making finished goods just in time to be sent to the buyer
- receiving raw materials and other stock items just in time for production
- making part of the finished product just in time for it to be used in the next production process.

If JIT is to work successfully, few errors can be made. JIT therefore often operates as part of a <u>total</u> <u>quality</u> <u>management</u> (TQM) system.

QUALITY AND STOCK CONTROL

OPTIMUM STOCK

Managers will calculate the optimum – best – stock level. This is the level that <u>reduces</u> <u>costs</u> <u>to</u> <u>a</u> <u>minimum</u>. They will take into account:
- the <u>reorder level</u> – the stock level at which a new order will be made
- the <u>minimum stock level</u> – the 'buffer' stock, which, in a 'just-in-time' system, is at or near zero
- the <u>maximum stock</u> – the highest level of stock
- the <u>reorder quantity</u> – the most economical number to order at any one time.

An <u>economic order quantity</u> (EOQ) can be calculated by comparing the costs of holding stock with the savings available through bulk-buying.

QUICK TEST

1. Costs of holding high stocks include large s_____ costs, and the risk of the stock becoming o____ o____ d____ . The costs of holding low stocks include the risk of being o____ o____ s_____ , and therefore losing c_____.

2. Explain the following: a) TQM

                             b) JIT

                             c) EOQ

2. a) a quality system that seeks to get things 'right first time'; b) a system used to minimise stock costs; c) the most economic quantity to reorder.

1. storage, out of date, out of stock, custom(ers).

EXAM QUESTIONS — Use the questions to test your progress. Check your answers on page 95.

1. The job method of production is used to make:
a) newspapers ☐
b) bridges ☐
c) televisions ☐
d) vacuum cleaners. ☐

2. Which of the following form part of the production function?

Undertaking quality control	Producing questionnaires
Measuring productivity	Inducting new staff
Producing invoices	Undertaking personal selling

3. Link these terms with their descriptions.

a) Lean production — i) The level to which stock must fall to trigger a new order
b) Just-in-time — ii) The number of stock items ordered
c) Buffer stock — iii) An approach used to minimise waste and overcome some of the problems of mass production
d) Reorder level — iv) A system for delivering more stock to production just before it runs out
e) Reorder quantity — v) A check to see if quality standards are being met
f) Quality control — vi) A 'reserve' stock level held in case of problems

4. a) Link these terms with their description and with the most appropriate illustration.

Economy	Description	Illustration
1) Concentration	a) specialist managers	i) Cornish pasties
2) Purchasing	b) good name of the area	ii) joint research venture
3) Reputation	c) specialist advertising	iii) skilled labour force
4) Technical	d) using specialist machinery	iv) discounts on raw materials
5) Marketing	e) cheaper money	v) advertising agency employed
6) Information	f) industry located in a limited area	vi) HRM manager
7) Managerial	g) businesses share research	vii) paying lower interest rates
8) Financial	h) buying in bulk	viii) CAD/CAM machines

b) Identify the external economies of scale in the above list.

....

5. Supercuddle Ltd is a company producing toys for a specialist, collectors' market. Some toys are made individually by hand, and others are produced as 'limited editions'.
a) Identify the most appropriate production method used

i) to make toys individually

....

ii) to make 'limited edition' toys.

....

b) Give **three** reasons why Supercuddle Ltd may find it cheaper to produce the limited edition toys.

....
....
....

6. These are the possible output figures for Watchit Ltd, a company making and selling computer screens.

Expected yearly sales (000)	Unit cost price (£)	Unit selling price (£)
5	45	60
6	44	57
7	42	55
8	40	52
9	41	50

a) How do these figures show that Watchit Ltd gains from economies of scale?

....
....

b) Suggest **two** economies of scale which you would expect this company to have. Give reasons for your choice.

....
....

c) The directors have decided to sell their screens for £52 each. Explain why you think they have chosen this figure.

....
....
....

7. Go-Low Plc is a company that produces various low-calorie food agents for use in sweet foodstuffs such as chocolate and ice cream. The low-calorie product is used as a sugar substitute. Go-Low Plc uses both mass (flow-line) and batch production methods to make its products. The company is aware of the importance of good quality systems. The directors have introduced a Total Quality Management (TQM) system in the company.

a) i) Explain, with an example of each, the difference between batch production and mass production.

....
....
....

ii) Compare the suitability of each of these production methods for making low-calorie food agents (artificial sweeteners).

....
....

b) i) Explain the meaning of 'Total Quality Management'.

....
....
....

ii) How might this system apply to a company such as Go-Low PLC?

....
....

How did you do?

1–2	correct	.start again
3–4	correct	.getting there
5–6	correct	.good work
all 7	correct	.excellent

advertising primary data special offer brands life cycle research

MARKETING IN BUSINESS

A market consists of people – buyers and sellers – who are trading in a product. The price is normally set by the supply of, and the demand for, the product. The market for any business consists of its actual and its potential customers. This market may be local (e.g. a street market), national (the mass market) or international. Markets can be classified as:

- *consumer markets – goods and services bought by the general public*
- *industrial markets – machinery and equipment used in business, and business-related services (e.g. delivery, security).*

MARKETING AND THE MARKETING DEPARTMENT

Marketing is needed because people, businesses and advanced economies all specialise. The various goods and services supplied need to be sold. This takes place in a competitive environment. As a result, a business needs to discover:

- what to make and sell
- how many to make and sell
- who to sell to
- how to encourage these people to buy
- how much to charge for what is sold.

The role of the marketing department is to carry out marketing. This means it must link production to consumption. To do this, the department makes sure that the demands of its customers are met by what is being made. If the marketing department achieves this, it will meet customer wishes and help the business make a profit.

To do this, marketing staff must manage the marketing mix efficiently by:

- researching into the demand for the firm's products – e.g. through market research
- ensuring these products are competitive through pricing policies
- making sure they are available through efficient distribution
- keeping the products in the minds of its customers – by promoting them.

Marketing planning takes place to help the marketing department achieve its objectives. The existing position can be analysed using a SWOT analysis. This analyses:

- underline{S} – the business's present strengths
- underline{W} – and weaknesses
- underline{O} – its market opportunities
- underline{T} – and the external threats it faces.

MARKET SEGMENTATION

A market is segmented by dividing it into different parts (segments). When this is carried out, the business may concentrate on one, several or all the different segments. If the business concentrates on one segment only, this is its <u>niche</u> market. These markets are normally for specialist, or limited demand, items.

- <u>Sex</u> – marketers target certain products (e.g. some drinks) at either men or women.

- <u>Age</u> – e.g. fashion clothing and music aimed at the youth market.

- <u>Ethnicity</u> – people with different backgrounds have different wants, e.g. religious beliefs and cultural tastes regarding food.

There are different ways to <u>segment</u> a market.

- <u>Population</u> – its size and distribution varies, and regional tastes also differ.

- <u>Income</u> and <u>social class</u> – e.g. 'luxury' goods and high-price cars aimed at wealthier consumers.

- <u>Lifestyle</u> – e.g. sports and exercise goods and services.

Mothercare

Marks and Spencer

Next

Segmenting the market helps the marketing department to <u>understand</u> <u>its</u> <u>market</u>. It allows the business to target:

- the <u>product</u> in each segment by establishing its <u>USP</u> (Unique Selling Point), the feature that distinguishes this product from others
- its <u>advertising</u> and other forms of promotion in the segment.

QUICK TEST

1. List four different ways to segment a consumer market.
2. The 'marketing mix' consists of: p_____, p_____, d_____ (or p_____) and p_____.
3. State one possible strength, weakness, opportunity and threat for a business you have studied.

1. Age; sex; income/social class; lifestyle
2. Product, price, distribution (place), promotion
3. (e.g. McDonald's) strength, known brand; weakness, coping with orders at peak times; opportunity, expansion through franchising; threat, increasing demand for vegetarian foods.

MARKET RESEARCH

PRIMARY DATA (INFORMATION)

This data does not already exist. It is obtained from **surveys**, which involve studying and questioning a section of the market. It is usually impossible or too expensive to use the whole market, and so a **sample** is selected. This sample should **reflect** (be representative of) **the whole market**.

Research used to obtain primary data may be either quantitative or qualitative.
- **Quantitative** research summarises the findings in the form of **figures**. For example, in a survey, 'closed' questions such as 'how many ...?' or 'which of these ...?' will be asked.
- **Qualitative** research studies consumer's **behaviour**.
- In a survey 'open' questions will be set, e.g. to find out reasons for buying, and opinions about the product.

There are many different methods used to collect primary data.

INTERVIEWS
These take place either face-to-face (usually for products in consumer markets) or by telephone (often for industrial market products).
- Information can be obtained **quickly**, and the interviewer can **explain questions** if necessary.
- **Questionnaires** have to be designed carefully, and it can be an **expensive** method of collecting data.

POSTAL SURVEYS
These are popular alternatives to personal interviews.
- This is normally **less expensive** than conducting interviews, and a wide **geographical area** can be sampled.
- The postal survey may have only a **low response** rate, and **points cannot be clarified**.

CONSUMER PANELS
These groups of people meet to discuss the market or product being researched.
- Different types of panel can be used: e.g. **product** panels obtain views on new products, and **buying** panels are used to obtain information on buying habits.

OBSERVATION
The actions of consumers in the market-place are observed, e.g. using cameras placed in shops.
- This gives more **objective** evidence.
- Observing people behave in the way they do **will not explain** their behaviour.

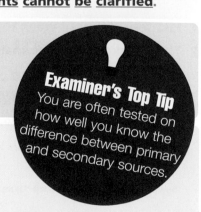

Examiner's Top Tip
You are often tested on how well you know the difference between primary and secondary sources.

SECONDARY DATA INFORMATION

This comes from <u>existing</u> <u>sources</u>, those that have already been published. It is widely known as <u>desk</u> <u>research</u>, because the information can be obtained by sitting at a desk. Information from <u>inside</u> the business can be used, for example:

*   sales and production figures
*   the cost of advertising and marketing campaigns
*   selling and distribution costs.

Information from <u>external</u> sources can also be used. The <u>government</u> often supplies most of this information. The government's <u>Office</u> <u>for</u> <u>National</u> <u>Statistics</u> (ONS) produces many relevant publications, including:

*   Regional Trends – e.g. population movements taking place within the UK
*   Social Trends – e.g. how consumer spending is changing
*   Economic Trends – this summarises the changes taking place in the economy
*   Annual Abstract of Statistics – a summary of the UK economy, e.g. wages and prices.

Published information is also available from many other sources. These sources include:

*   banks
*   chambers of commerce
*   the TUC and the CBI
*   professional associations
*   newspapers.

Examiner's Top Tip
Remember that secondary data can also be obtained from inside a business.

Examiner's Top Tip
Memorise one or two examples of government statistics.

KEY POINTS

The role of <u>market</u> <u>research</u> is to get information about the market(s) in which the business operates. This is one part of <u>marketing</u> <u>research</u>, which also includes research into:

*   the <u>product</u> – e.g. its price and its packaging
*   the <u>promotion</u> – e.g. if the best advertising media are being used.

When we compare primary and secondary data:

*   primary data is obtained <u>exclusively</u> for the business
*   it is therefore <u>more</u> <u>appropriate</u> for the needs of the business but, because it needs collecting 'from scratch', it is much more <u>costly</u> than secondary data and takes longer to collect
*   although secondary data is cheaper and quicker to obtain, it has the major disadvantage that it is <u>not</u> <u>designed</u> <u>for</u> <u>the</u> <u>needs</u> <u>of</u> <u>the</u> <u>business</u>.

INTERNET
The original market research group.
www.mori.com

QUICK TEST

1. **Why is sampling used to collect primary data?**
2. **Popular ways of collecting primary data are to use f_____ t____ f_____ i_____, t_____ s_____ and p_____ s_____.**
3. **List three sources of secondary data, other than the UK government.**

3. Local chambers of commerce, banks, the CBI.
2. Face-to-face interviews, telephone surveys, postal surveys.
1. Impossible or too expensive to research the whole market.

PRODUCT

THE PRODUCT MIX

Most businesses sell more than one product. The range of products they sell is known as the 'product mix'. The product mix for any business is influenced by the **number** of **market segments** it sells in. The **Boston Matrix** ('Boston Box') is one technique used to analyse the product mix.

- **Stars** – these products have a high market share in a fast-growing market, but still need much investment to turn them into Cash Cows.
- **Cash Cows** – with a high market share in mature markets, these are the business's most valuable products.
- **Problem Children** – these products have a low market share in a high-growth market, and need further investment if they are to become successful.
- **Dogs** – these have a low market share in a low-growth market, and are unprofitable (or loss-making).

THE PRODUCT LIFE-CYCLE

This analyses the various parts of a product's life. All products have a life-cycle.

- After being developed, the product is introduced on to the market.
- This <u>Introduction</u> stage is associated with high advertising and other costs, with the product making a loss because of this.
- More consumers start buying the product in the <u>Growth</u> stage; it increases its market share, establishes brand loyalty and becomes profitable.
- The product has its maximum sales and profits during the <u>Maturity</u> stage; it reaches market saturation and/or faces increasing competition.
- It goes into <u>Decline</u>, with falling sales and market share.

Because it is so difficult to create successful products, businesses often try to extend the life of these products. These <u>EXTENSION STRATEGIES</u> include:

- changing its <u>USE</u> – e.g. selling ice-cream forms of popular chocolate bars
- changing its <u>PACKAGING</u> – e.g. using it to emphasise a 'new improved model' approach.

Examiner's Top Tip
Remember that the life-cycle shows successful products only: most fail at or before the Introduction stage.

KEY POINTS

Broad links can be made between the product life-cycle and the 'Boston Box'.

LIFE-CYCLE			BOSTON BOX
Introduction	⟷	Problem Child	
Growth	⟷	Star	
Maturity	⟷	Cash Cow	
Decline	⟷	Dog	

Examiner's Top Tip
Learn some real-life examples of products whose lives have been extended.

BRANDING

By branding its product, the business guarantees to the consumer that the next one bought will be virtually the same as the last one.

- **This encourages <u>repeat</u> <u>purchases</u> through brand loyalty.**
- **Branding also helps the business <u>differentiate</u> – make different – its products from those of its competitors.**
- **The business can use the brand's <u>unique</u> <u>selling</u> <u>point</u> (USP) to increase sales.**
- **<u>Mass</u> <u>advertising</u> becomes possible with branding.**

QUICK TEST

1. Group the stages below under their correct headings:

   BOSTON BOX   **LIFE CYCLE**

   Maturity, Cash Cow, Growth,

   Decline, Dog, Star, Introduction,

   Problem Child

2. Identify two strategies used to extend the life of a product.

3. What is the 'product mix'?

3. The range of products marketed by the business.
2. Changes in use; changes in packaging.
1. Boston Box: Cash Cow, Dog, Star, Problem Child;   Life-cycle: Introduction, Growth, Maturity, Decline.

PRICING TACTICS

The marketing department may use different pricing tactics to sell products.

· <u>Psychological</u> pricing – a price is set just below a significant whole number, e.g. £9.95 rather than £10.00.

· <u>Capturing</u> pricing – when a business makes both the 'hardware' and 'software' elements of a product (e.g. Nintendo, Sony and Sega game products), it may sell the hardware at a low price so that it can 'capture' the long-term sales on its high-priced software items.

· <u>Discrimination</u> pricing – the business sets different prices in different segments (e.g. railway <u>off-peak</u> and <u>young-person</u> fares are much lower than full-priced fares for the same journey).

· <u>Special</u> <u>offer</u> pricing – e.g. a 'two for the price of one' tactic is used by shops to encourage into the store customers who are then likely to buy other items.

· <u>Loss</u> <u>leaders</u> – some products may be sold by stores at near or below their cost price, again to tempt shoppers to enter the store.

Examiner's Top Tip
Point out in your answers that a pricing policy must balance profitability with the need to remain competitive.

DEMAND-BASED PRICING

The basic law of supply and demand is that <u>demand</u> <u>falls</u> <u>as</u> <u>price</u> <u>increases</u> and <u>demand</u> <u>increases</u> <u>as</u> <u>price</u> <u>falls</u>. Price is therefore a major influence on the level of demand for the products of a business. Other influences on a product's demand include:

• the availability of <u>substitutes</u> for the business's product – the more substitutes there are available, the more sensitive the product will be to changes in its price (consumers will switch to the substitutes)

• the level of <u>consumer</u> <u>income</u> – in general, demand for a product increases as income levels increase

• changes in consumer <u>tastes</u> – demand will change as tastes change

• how <u>sensitive</u> customers are to price – they balance the price against other aspects, e.g. the product's status, quality, design and performance.

Examiner's Top Tip
Some questions expect you to show an understanding of the link between prices, profits and survival.

COST-BASED PRICING

Accountants can calculate the <u>full</u> <u>cost</u> of making a product. Many businesses take this full-cost figure, and then include a <u>mark-up</u> so that a profit will be made.

• *The main limitation of using this cost-based pricing is that it <u>ignores</u> <u>the</u> <u>competition</u>.*
• *Most businesses are <u>price</u> <u>takers</u>, not <u>price</u> <u>leaders</u>.*
• *Price takers must set prices close to others in the market.*
• *If the business uses cost-based pricing only, it may find competitors' prices are lower.*
• *In such cases, it will not be able to compete successfully on price.*

profit

distribution

admin

labour

raw materials

PRICING STRATEGIES FOR NEW PRODUCTS

Businesses use different strategies to price their new products. Incorrect pricing strategies mean the business will <u>not</u> <u>find</u> <u>customers</u> and therefore will <u>lose</u> <u>income</u>.

PENETRATION PRICING
- A <u>low</u> <u>price</u> is set in the hope of gaining a high market share.
- The business will gain <u>economies</u> <u>of</u> <u>scale</u>, which help it keep the price low.
- The low price set may stop competitors from entering this market.

SKIMMING (OR CREAMING)
- The business brings out a new, unique product, which is the early <u>market</u> <u>leader</u>.
- This enables it to set a <u>high</u> <u>price</u> because there is no competition.
- The price falls when competitors with similar products enter the market.

QUICK TEST

1. State the pricing tactic that describes the following:

   a) 'Buy one, get one free'

   b) 'For sale, £4990'.

c) 'Hair cutting and styling for senior citizens, half-price every Thursday'.

2. Delete the incorrect alternatives: penetration pricing is a high-cost/low-cost strategy used for new products/existing products.

3. List three influences on the demand for a product.

3. Consumer income levels, consumer tastes, consumer sensitivity to price.
2. Delete 'high-cost' and 'existing' products.
1. a) Special offer pricing; b) psychological pricing; c) discrimination pricing.

distributing the product

PLACE

DISTRIBUTION

Place is that part of the marketing mix that deals with distributing a business's products. Costs of distribution include warehousing, stockholding and transport.
- The business must get its products in the <u>right</u> <u>amounts</u> to the <u>right</u> <u>market</u> and at the <u>right</u> <u>time</u>, using the <u>right</u> <u>channel</u> of distribution.

Selecting the distribution channel is influenced by:
- the scale of the <u>business</u> – large-scale businesses usually do their own distribution, e.g. owning their own transport fleet
- the type of <u>market</u> – e.g. a manufacturer selling goods nationally usually needs the support of both wholesalers and retailers
- the <u>product</u> – e.g. specialist goods with a limited demand often use direct channels
- the need to balance the channel's <u>cost</u> against its <u>efficiency</u> in getting the product to the consumer.

DISTRIBUTION CHANNELS

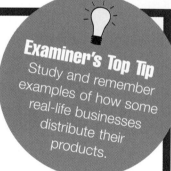

Examiner's Top Tip
Study and remember examples of how some real-life businesses distribute their products.

These 'channels' are the routes the product follows from the business to the consumer. A business may choose from a number of different routes.

① THROUGH WHOLESALER AND RETAILER TO CONSUMER
- This is the traditional route for consumer goods.
- Agents may be used rather than wholesalers, e.g. in overseas markets.

② THROUGH WHOLESALER TO CONSUMER
- This channel is sometimes used in high-population areas to sell consumer durables and other expensive items.

③ THROUGH RETAILER TO CONSUMER
- Producers often sell directly to the large-scale retailers that have their own large warehouses and who carry out their own wholesale function.
- Some producers set up (e.g. by franchising) their own retail outlets and sell their products using this distribution method.

④ DIRECT TO CONSUMER
- This direct selling route is often used by producers of industrial goods.
- It is becoming more popular in consumer goods markets (e.g. factory outlets, mail-order catalogues, leaflets through the post).

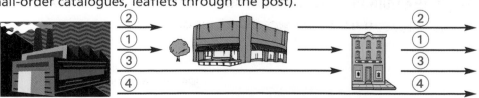

WHOLESALERS

Wholesalers are not as commonly used as they once were. A major reason for this is the growth of large-scale retailing.

- Major retailers such as Tesco and Sainsbury have their own warehousing and distribution systems.
- The fall in the number of small-scale retailers has also affected wholesalers.
- Wholesalers have adapted, e.g. by setting up voluntary chains and supplying these linked retailers with their goods.

Traditional wholesalers still offer valuable services to both producers and retailers.

Services to the producer:
- buying and storing in bulk – this cuts the producer's distribution costs
- advice and promotion – feedback on the product's popularity can be given, and the wholesaler may help promote the manufacturer's product
- taking on risk – the wholesaler bears the risk of not selling the products.

Services to the retailer:
- breaking bulk – the wholesaler 'buys big' and 'sells small', cutting the retailer's storage costs
- information and choice – product information may be given on a variety of goods
- delivery and credit – many wholesalers still offer a delivery service for the smaller retailer, and their credit facilities help retailers finance their purchases.

E-COMMERCE

Electronic commerce (e-commerce) is a popular development, now used by many businesses to sell their products. E-commerce options include selling over the Internet, or using electronic shopping malls available through interactive television.

Advantages to the business of using e-commerce include:
- *consumers can buy products 24 hours a day, seven days a week*
- *it can be inexpensive to set up and operate*
- *since the Internet is international, the business can sell in new markets.*

Problems of e-commerce include:
- *many consumers lack the technology or expertise*
- *a lack of trust in buying over the Internet*
- *customers may simply be unaware of the e-commerce site.*

INTERNET

www.buyguide.co.uk
www.ukshoppingzone.co.uk
www.shop.co.uk
www.first-e.com
www.halifax-online.co.uk
www.smile.co.uk

QUICK TEST

1. Tick the correct column:

	Service to producer	Service to retailer
a) Breaking bulk	☐	☐
b) Buying in bulk	☐	☐
c) Taking on risk	☐	☐
d) Offering credit	☐	☐

2. Products are needed in the right m_____ in the right a_____ at the right t_____. To do this, the right c_____ must be selected and used.

1. a) retailer; b) producer c) producer d) retailer
2. Market, amount, time, channel

You can do it if you B&Q it

Gotta catch 'em all

Wazzaaaap..!

PROMOTING BY ADVERTISING

Search for the Rowntree

Feed the Tango inside

Because I'm worth it

That's Asda price

Vauxhall: raising the standard

WHY BUSINESSES ADVERTISE

Advertising:
- informs customers who otherwise may not find out about the product
- increases sales, which increases production and may bring about economies of scale
- encourages competition, which keeps prices down
- supports other industries (e.g. many newspapers survive through advertising revenue)

Advertising can be criticised for exploiting people by tempting them to buy:
- things they do not need
- what they cannot afford
- items that may do them harm (e.g. tobacco).

Advertising sets out to inform and persuade. It must be paid for by a sponsor. It is often directed at a mass audience, and therefore may use mass media such as newspapers, TV and radio.

A business pays for advertising to:
- compete – competitive advertising tries to counter the advertising of competitors
- increase its sales – e.g. in a new market segment
- launch new products – customers need to find out about these
- improve its image – this 'corporate' or 'institution' advertising promotes the business name.

Examiner's Top Tip
It is worth remembering that many adverts are part persuasive and part informative.

PERSUASIVE AND INFORMATIVE ADVERTISING

PERSUASIVE ADVERTISING
- *This form seeks to make customers believe that they need the business's product.*
- *It often tries to tempt consumers to buy the business's brand rather than the brands of its competitors.*
- *Most mass-media advertising is persuasive.*

please buy me!

INFORMATIVE ADVERTISING
- *This form of advertising sets out to give customers information.*
- *It is often carried out by government and public bodies (public service advertising).*

this is me

ADVERTISING MEDIA

Examiner's Top Tip
Make sure you can explain the difference between advertising and other forms of promotion.

BROADCAST MEDIA
These mass-market media are very popular, but can be very costly.
- TV advertising offers <u>colour</u>, <u>sound</u> <u>and</u> <u>movement</u>. It is the <u>most</u> <u>expensive</u> form of advertising, and only the larger companies tend to advertise on national television.
- Commercial radio is <u>less</u> <u>costly</u>, but <u>lacks</u> <u>visual</u> <u>impact</u> and has a <u>smaller</u> <u>audience</u>.
- The cinema can be used, for example, to <u>target</u> <u>groups</u> (e.g. the audience often has a high proportion of young people).

PRINT-BASED MEDIA
If it decides to use print-based media, the business can choose from national (daily and Sunday papers, monthly magazines), local (local papers) and specialist media (special-interest magazines).
- The advert is in a <u>permanent</u> <u>form</u>, and can be cut out and kept for future reference.
- It can also be linked with <u>other</u> <u>promotion</u> <u>forms</u>, e.g. competitions (sales promotion).
- These adverts can often give <u>more</u> <u>information</u> than adverts in other forms of media.
- Advertising in special-interest magazines means a business can sell to a <u>specialist</u> <u>market</u>.
- The advert tends to <u>lack</u> <u>impact</u> compared with broadcast media, since there is no sound and/or movement.

OUTDOOR MEDIA
- Posters are a popular form of outdoor advertising, attracting a <u>large</u> <u>audience</u> (e.g. placed by busy roads).
- Illuminated signs are widely used in city centres, again attracting a large audience for little cost.

Examiner's Top Tip
You may have to select appropriate advertising media for a given product: be realistic (do not select national TV advertising for a local car boot sale!).

QUICK TEST

1. Advertising is p_____ for by a s_____ , and uses m_____ m_____ directed at a m_____ a_____ .

2. List three reasons why a business chooses to advertise

3. Suggest a suitable advertising medium for the following:

a) a local carnival is to take place

b) a new washing powder is to be launched

c) a political party wants to attack another party at a general election.

3. a) local radio/local paper/leaflet in paper or through door;   b) national TV;   c) roadside poster.
2. Compete with others, inform customers of new products, increase market share.
1. paid, sponsor, mass media, mass audience.

OTHER TYPES OF PROMOTION

SALES PROMOTION

Examiner's Top Tip
You can use the term 'below-the-line' promotion to summarise these methods.

These methods are used when marketers decide to promote their products by directly encouraging people to buy them. This is often achieved by offering <u>incentives</u> to buy. <u>Branding</u> and <u>packaging</u> are other important influences in sales promotion campaigns.

POINT-OF-SALE (POS) DISPLAY
* Also known as <u>merchandising</u>, this method promotes the product <u>where</u> <u>it</u> <u>is</u> <u>sold</u>.
* Examples include using 'dump bins' by the till to sell sweets, encouraging impulse buying.

PROMOTION INCENTIVES
* These incentives tempt the consumer to buy particular brands.
* They are commonly used by supermarkets and by producers whose goods are sold in them.
* Examples include multi-pack and money-off offers, price reductions, free gifts, competitions, and 'proof of purchase' refunds.

OTHER FORMS OF SALES PROMOTION
* <u>Exhibitions</u> are used to promote both consumer and industrial goods.
* <u>Sponsorship</u> and '<u>corporate</u> <u>entertainment</u>' are often linked with major sporting events, and are used by larger businesses to promote their image.
* Offers of <u>after-sales</u> <u>service</u> and <u>guarantees</u> are often used in encouraging consumers to buy particular brands of products.

DIRECT MARKETING

Direct marketing methods are often used for <u>niche</u> <u>market</u> <u>products</u>. These methods involve direct approaches to the customer, and include:
* the use of <u>mail</u> <u>order</u> <u>catalogues</u>
* 'personal' letters and other <u>direct</u> <u>mail</u> ('junk mail') through the post to potential customers.

PERSONAL SELLING

www.tradeworld.co.uk/exhibitions

This involves <u>face-to-face</u> <u>contact</u> between the salesperson and the customer. It includes the traditional door-to-door milk delivery and is also used to sell industrial goods. Although this is a <u>labour-intensive</u> and <u>costly</u> method, it offers several benefits:
- the salesperson can adjust the sales 'pitch' or offer sales promotional materials to <u>persuade</u> <u>the</u> <u>customer</u> to buy
- the customer can <u>ask</u> <u>questions</u> and the salesperson can offer a <u>demonstration</u>
- the salesperson can <u>provide</u> <u>technical</u> <u>information</u> if necessary.

PUBLIC RELATIONS

Although this is not a true form of promotion, public relations (PR) is often linked with it. Unlike advertising, <u>publicity</u> is not paid for by the business. The purpose of PR is to <u>improve</u> <u>relations</u> between a business and the public. To do this it:
- *issues <u>press</u> <u>releases</u> to publicise good points about the business*
- *supports any '<u>institution</u>' advertising the business carries out.*

Examiner's Top Tip
Remember that publicity is not paid for, a fact which distinguishes it from advertising.

KEY POINTS

The <u>AIDA</u> approach is often used in promotion campaigns, especially for expensive items:
- the campaign attempts to capture the <u>attention</u> of would-be purchasers
- it tries to <u>interest</u> them in buying the product
- it creates a <u>desire</u> to own it
- this should lead to the <u>action</u> of buying the product.

With all forms of promotion, the business will <u>measure</u> <u>the</u> <u>cost</u> <u>against</u> <u>the</u> <u>benefit</u>.

QUICK TEST

1. Tick the relevant column:

	Sales promotion	Personal selling	Direct marketing	Public relations
a) Junk mail	☐	☐	☐	☐
b) Visit by a salesman	☐	☐	☐	☐
c) Issuing a press release	☐	☐	☐	☐
d) Buy one get one free	☐	☐	☐	☐

2. An AIDA promotion campaign concentrates on creating a_____, i_____, d_____ and a_____.

3. Name four different methods of sales promotion

3. POS display, promotion incentives, exhibitions, sponsorship.
2. Attention, interest, desire, action.
1. a) direct marketing; b) personal selling; c) PR; d) sales promotion.

1. Analysing the market in order to identify different types of consumers is known as market _____ , and finding out their preferences is called market _____.

2. One of the four Ps in the marketing mix is:
a) profit ☐
b) product ☐
c) pollution ☐
d) piece rate ☐

3. Which of these are examples of secondary (desk) research?
a) looking at the firm's sales statistics ☐
b) observing people doing their shopping ☐
c) carrying out opinion polls ☐
d) surveying people by telephone ☐
e) reading government-produced statistics. ☐

4. Which of the following are the responsibility of the marketing department?
a) Interviewing job applicants ☐
b) Buying new machinery ☐
c) Undertaking market research ☐
d) Planning how products are to be distributed ☐
e) Carrying out sales promotion ☐
f) Inspecting newly made products ☐
g) Buying raw materials ☐
h) Selling surplus equipment ☐

5. Name one suitable advertising medium for each of the following:
a) a new GCSE Business Studies textbook ....
b) a used Playstation ....
c) a new mobile phone. ....

6. The PrettyPong range of cleaning products is made by Worth Ltd.. The directors wish to introduce a 'new, environmentally-friendly PrettyPong' kitchen worktop and sink cleaning product. They hope to establish quickly a large market share in this highly competitive market.
   The Marketing Director of Worth Ltd has been asked to suggest whether the company should use skimming or penetration pricing for the new product, and how it should be promoted.
a) Outline why branding is important to Worth Ltd.

....

b) i) Explain the terms 'skimming' and 'penetration'.

....
....

ii) Suggest which of these two strategies should be used for the new product. Give reasons for your answer.

....
....

c) Explain how the directors will need to consider advertising when marketing the new product.

....

d) Select **two** sales promotion methods the directors might use for the new product. Justify your choice.

....
....

7. Store-it Ltd manufactures and sells desks and storage units for home computers. These are sold directly by the company, as well as in major 'out-of-town' computer stores. The chart below shows the product life cycle for its 'TidyUp' product range.

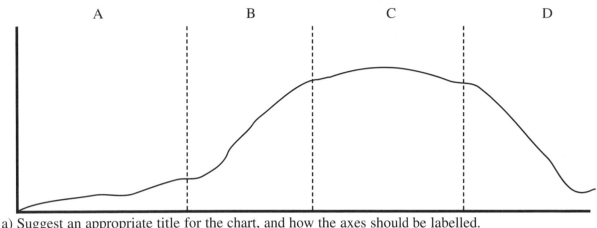

a) Suggest an appropriate title for the chart, and how the axes should be labelled.

....
....
....

b) i) Name each stage A, B, C and D.

....
....
....
....

ii) Describe what happens at each stage.

....
....
....
....

c) How might Store-it Ltd attempt to extend the life of its product ranges?

....
....
....

d) How might Store-it Ltd use market research to discover who is buying its products?

....
....
....
....
....
....

How did you do?

1–2	correct	....start again
3–4	correct	....getting there
5–6	correct	....good work
all 7	correct	....excellent

Our Economy and Businesses

1. House builder; car manufacturer; food-processing firm.
2. d) Labour.
3. The owners are limited to the amount they can lose in the business.
4. a) partnership; b) sole trader; c) partnership; d) public company;
   e) private company.
5. Price set by demand and supply. If demand exceeds supply, price rises, encouraging suppliers to mak more and consumers to demand less. If supply exceeds demand, price falls, encouraging suppliers to make less and consumers to demand more. In both cases, eventually demand and supply reach 'equilibrium'.
6. a) Limited liability to protect the owners financially; separate legal existence, so the business can continue more easily if one of the owners leaves.
   b) The company's business affairs would remain more private; very costly
   to set up a PLC; owners risk losing direct control of the company
7. a) i) Franchisee; ii) Franchisor.
   b) Advantages of receiving specialist support from franchisor, and being able to sell a range of recognised products; disadvantages of losing some control over business matters, and having to pay some profits to the franchisor.
   c) Survival; make an adequate profit.
   d) The petrol company will probably have objectives based on market share and keeping its shareholders contented.
8. a) Secondary sector, private sector
   b) i) Shareholders, local community
   ii) Shareholders are interested in the company's profitability and the security of their investment; local community in environmental matters and how the company supports their community (e.g. employment)
   c) Benefits: wider market (more sales and profits), diversifying into different markets (safer). Problems: setting up how to sell (getting information, channels of distribution), different language/culture (marketing problems), risk of failing to sell products in new markets (financial problems), having to face local competition, dealing in other currencies (UK not in Single Currency zone).
   d) Single market in EU (standard paperwork, no tariffs, easier procedures).
   e) Cost of land – more expensive in south-east England. Location to market – closer to rest of Europe, but may be further away from UK-based customers. Effect on employees – can/will they move with the company? Financing the move – how will the money be found?

Inside and Outside the Business

1. d) organisation chart.
2. c) laws.
3. a) advantage; b) advantage or disadvantage; c) disadvantage; d) advantage; e) disadvantage
4. Horizontal a) and e); vertical forwards b); vertical backwards d); lateral c).
5. i) b; ii) f; iii) e; iv) a; v) c; vi) e; vii) d
6. Greater control over outlets, and therefore marketing and pricing policy. Greater control over supply, therefore more secure position all profits made at all stages belong to the business.
7. Advantages: common external tariff benefits those trading within the market; freedom of movement means bigger markets; EU labour source available to UK firms; free movement of capital means inward investment in the UK and its businesses.
   Disadvantages: free movement also introduces more competition into the UK; competing with firms using the single currency; skilled labour may leave for other EU countries.
8. a) Purchasing, technical support, maintenance.
   b) To deal with existing and potential staff; to recruit new staff (recruitment manager); to support existing staff (staff welfare manager); to train, negotiate with and administer staff (managers plus office staff).

c) hierarchy: formal structure shown by the various levels in the chart; span of control: number of people under the control of one person, e.g. Production Controller's span includes Production Office staff; chain of command: control through the hierarchy, e.g. Financial Director to Accounts Office Manager, to Accounts Office staff.
   d) Clarifies the formal hierarchy and decision-making process; acts as a record; can use when inducting new staff to explain structure.
   e) i) Paying wages/salaries to new starters.
   ii) Memo: stating details of new starter and pay rate; email: to confirm payment made.
   iii) Reduces misunderstanding inside and outside the company; allows ideas and information to be transmitted efficiently; the more efficient communication is, the more profitable the company is likely to be.

People in Business

1. Recruiting staff; keeping staff records; organising staff training
2. c) a short-list
3. c) job description
4. a) self-actualisation (or ego); (b) social; (c) basic; (d) safety
5. Decide what the training priorities are; analyse the jobs for which training is to be given; prepare training requirements; select the people to be trained.
6. a) i) New ideas introduced.
   ii) Pay rates (competitive?); job prospects (promotion?); working conditions (pleasant?); number of people who can meet demands of the job (qualifications/skills?).
   b) i) Overview of company history; tour of premises; meeting with staff from the department.
   ii) new member feels motivated; makes an early contribution to the work.
   c) External certificate/qualification likely; gaining wider knowledge and skills.
7. a) Identify feelings and wishes of members; negotiate with management to meet members' wishes.
   b) Improving working conditions: e.g. hours of work, holidays, physical conditions.
   c) Work-to-rule: employees follow the rule book precisely, which normally slows up production. Overtime ban: refuse to work above contracted hours, which may affect production and meeting any urgent orders.
   d) Conciliation – meeting both parties to find 'common ground' to resolve dispute; arbitration – independent third party makes decision; on dispute information/advice – expertise offered.
8. a) Asks for young 'man', not 'person'.
   b) Hours; location of work; contact address/phone number.
   c) i) Time rate (overtime mentioned).
   ii) Annual salary with or without commission/bonus on sales made.

Finance in Business

1. Calculating financial ratios; preparing financial statements.
2. d) Output
3. c) Production figures
4. b) Creditors
5. A profit and loss account; a cash flow statement.
6. Cost of borrowing: how much, and for how long?; length of time the finance is needed for: short-term, medium-term or long-term?
7. a) £51 000/200 = £255 each
   b) £52 000 – £51 000 = £1000 (£50 each)
   c) Fixed cost element is included in the average cost calculation and not the variable cost calculation.
8. Materials: exact amount to be bought not known, so flexible short-term finance such as an overdraft is necessary; van: long-term commitment needed, and important to know how much will be paid over how long, so long-term loan is suitable.
9. a) Profitability: return on capital employed (ROCE) 30/1500 = 2%; gross profit margin 150/600 = 25%, net profit margin 30/600 = 5% liquidity: current ratio 150 to 100 = 1.5 to 1; quick assets 100 to 100 = 1 to 1.

b) Profitability, 2p net profit from every £1 capital used to make this profit (very low return); 25p in the £ gross profit and 75p in the £ cost of sales; 5p in the £ net profit, liquidity, sufficient current assets, even excluding stock, to meet current liabilities.

c) Previous results, and/or competitors' results.

10. a) Contribution £3 – £1 (80p+20p) = £2
Break-even = fixed costs £8000 divided by £2 = 4000 T-shirts.

b) Break-even chart

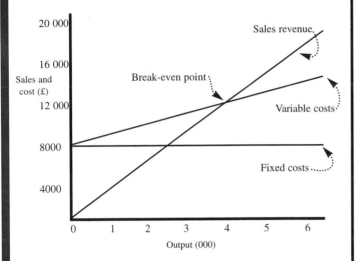

i) Break-even 4000; ii) break-even revenue £12 000 (proof: 4000 x £3); iii) profit £4000 (£18 000 – £14 000); iv) margin of safety 2000 units (6000 – 4000)

Making the Products

1. b) Bridges
2. Undertaking quality control, measuring productivity.
3. a) iii; b) iv; c) vi; d) i; e) ii; f) v
4. a) 1) f) iii; 2) h) iv; 3) b) i; 4) d) viii; 5) c) v; 6) g) ii; 7) a) vi; 8) e) vii
   b) Concentration, Reputation, Information.
5. a) i) Job, ii) batch.
   b) Greater chance of economies of scale (e.g. bulk buying); labour may be less skilled (less expensive); more machines may be used (quicker production).
6. a) The unit cost price falls as output increases.
   b) Purchasing economics: likely, e.g. due to bulk buying of components for the screens; technical economies: likely due to specialist manufacturing equipment needed for computer screens.
   c) After 8000, diseconomies of scale seem to start (unit cost rises to £41). 8000 also gives maximum profit:
   £12 (selling less cost) x 8000 = £96 000, largest figure obtainable (next largest = £13 x 7000 = £91 000).
7. a) i) Batch: set number of products made, before production switches to another model, e.g. baking batches of different loaves of bread; mass: one production line devoted exclusively to making a single product, e.g. mass-produced chocolate bars.
   ii) Either could be suitable, depending on demand. Mass production if sweeteners sold nationally in bulk; batch production to meet particular orders from sweet/chocolate manufacturers.
   b) i) 'Get it right first time/more right next time' approach, where everyone is involved in continual improvement to his/her work.
   ii) Foodstuff production demands highest quality, so TQM appropriate. Employee involvement through, e.g. quality circles.

Selling the Products

1. Segmentation, research.
2. b) Product
3. a) and e)
4. Undertaking market research; carrying out sales promotion.
5. a) Leaflets from the publisher distributed to schools.
   b) Advert in a local paper.
   c) TV adverts.
6. a) Enables Worth Ltd to advertise and market the product; leads to repeat purchases from consumers; establishes brand loyalty.
   b) i) Skimming: sets high market price; penetration: sets low price.
   ii) Penetration: the market is already established, so the company is not first into the market and cannot be a price leader; a competitive market exists, and the company wants a high share of this; a low-price policy is therefore needed to encourage many consumers to buy.
   c) The directors need to do the following: identify which segments the company will focus on for marketing and advertising; select appropriate media from those available to the company; decide the extent to which the advertising will inform consumers, or persuade people to buy; establish an overall advertising strategy (e.g. which advertising agency to use); discuss how advertising is to be supported by other promotion methods.
   d) Free samples: allows consumers to try product, the sample could be supported by 'money off' coupon for first purchase or for another 'PrettyPong' product. Premium offers: e.g. consumer collects labels from first two purchases, sends label to company and receives another 'PrettyPong' product free. Both strategies encourage repeat purchases and/or promote other products in the range.
7. a) Title: Store-it Ltd. Product life cycle, TidyUp range. Vertical axis: Sales (£ or units). Horizontal axis: Time.
   b) i) A introduction, B growth, C maturity, D decline.
   ii) Introduction, product launched on market with low sales and high promotion and other expenditure; not established, and risk of failure. Growth, product being bought in greater numbers though still heavily promoted; repeat purchases and brand loyalty becoming established. Maturity, product at peak of sales; large market share and profits, but market gradually becoming saturated. Decline, sales and profits fall as other products become more competitive or interesting to consumers; heavy promotion, or attempt to extend life through various offers.
   c) Modifying the product in some way (e.g. new design, new colours); reducing price; selling in new market or new segment (e.g. as commercial office equipment).
   d) Primary (field) research: e.g. questionnaires, for customers at the computer stores or those buying directly from the company. Secondary (desk) research: e.g. studying statistics on computer sales, checking own sales data.

INDEX